D1603877

FICTION
UNBOXED

SEAN PLATT
JOHNNY B. TRUANT

FICTION UNBOXED

How Two Authors Wrote and Published a Book in 30 Days, From Scratch, In Front of the World.

by Sean Platt &
Johnny B. Truant

To our "Unboxers," who watched the story you're about to read unfold live.

Contents

Welcome to The Smarter Artist

THE SMARTER ARTIST IS A core part of the passionate publishing house, Sterling & Stone. Dedicated to helping authors and artists discover the intelligent yet hidden intersections that will help them build a business around their creativity, and get it to thrive before an ever growing audience.

Our hands-on, always transparent articulation of what is and isn't working for our own quickly growing publishing house offers a unique yet invaluable guide to creative entrepreneurs wanting to alchemize their ambitions into a healthy profit.

From launching our serials a year before Amazon's serial program, to hosting the rawest and most honest indie publishing podcast on the market, to writing a book live in 30 days, Sterling & Stone's three principal storytellers are always pioneering and getting smarter by the day.

The Smarter Artist is where they invite smart artists to get smarter by their side.

To get an early alert for the next book in our Smarter Artist series, occasional freebies, and exclusive Q&As, please visit the links at the end of this book.

A Note About This Book's Point of View

THIS BOOK HAS THREE AUTHORS: Sean Platt, Johnny B. Truant, and David Wright. That's because the three of us, working as hosts of the *Self-Publishing Podcast* and on behalf of our company Sterling & Stone, are kind of like the Three Musketeers: All for one and one for all. But less agile than the original Musketeers, and not nearly as adept with swords.

Fiction Unboxed (the live project version, conducted in June of 2014) was a team effort even though two of us were its prime movers. Sean and Johnny conducted the project and wrote the book that became *The Dream Engine*, while Dave acted as support crew and art department. That makes this book — the story of *Fiction Unboxed* and what any writer can learn from the experience — a team effort as well.

Dave gets a "with" credit on this book because his role is support rather than nose-to-grindstone. Sean (whose large nose dominates any grindstone) and Johnny will tell you this tale.

Even so, we thought the idea of writing this book using a "we" voice to accommodate two points of view would be distracting and awkward. As with our indie publishing guide, *Write. Publish. Repeat.*, we decided to tell this story from Johnny's POV.

(Side note: Simon Whistler, who will narrate the audiobook version, has a wonderful British accent. Johnny pushed to use his own POV because then everyone will continue to think he sounds like Simon.)

All "I" and "me" references in this book refer to Johnny ... but know that Sean is nearby, always half of the process (and forever ready to add his pair of pennies as he polishes the text after Johnny). Dave is in the background as well, mumbling from his hometown of [REDACTED] and telling us we're idiots.

How This Book is Organized

THIS BOOK TELLS THE STORY of a real, live, thirty-day writing project conducted in June of 2014 — a project called (you guessed it) *Fiction Unboxed*. During that live project, we decided that a cool way to add value for *Fiction Unboxed*'s original supporters would be to create *Fiction Unboxed: The Book Version*, which we rather undramatically referred to half the time by the less sexy name of "transcripts."

Because that was the plan, from the beginning: we'd finish the live project (which contained a whole lot of us meeting and talking as we wrote a new, full-length novel from scratch in front of a live audience), then we'd publish the transcripts as their own printed book.

It was a decent plan, and simultaneously the worst idea ever.

Sure, plenty of people prefer reading transcripts to watching video or listening to audio (and some people must, due to a hearing impairment), but they do so *knowing they're going to be reading transcripts of a live event*. No one wants to *buy a book off the shelf* and end up muddling through our verbal diarrhea. When you get a book, you want a *book*. You expect (and deserve) a coherent narrative; you want to learn in a logical order; you want to walk away smarter or more entertained than you were on page 1.

We ditched the idea of "just give them the transcripts" almost immediately. **We** *have* **provided the full** *Fiction Unboxed* **transcripts in a convenient e-book format via links**

at the back of this book, but dumping the transcripts with nothing else would have been cheating you. We decided the best way to frame *Fiction Unboxed: The Book* — the version you're reading now — would be to do what we do best.

We decided to tell you a story.

We had a tricky line to walk. We wanted to tell the tale of the thirty-day journey we shared with our audience of one thousand "Unboxers" as they watched us write a novel live. But simply "telling the story" felt masturbatory. You, the reader, need to leave this book having learned what *we* learned during the project. *Fiction Unboxed* showed the world that stories can come from nowhere, and that fiction writing is something you *do* rather than any sort of magic, birthright, or innate talent. It is something earned, not inherited.

We want you to be entertained by the *Fiction Unboxed* story, but more importantly we want you to learn a ton of lessons that will improve your abilities as a writer. And we hope you won't be passive, but will be inspired to action, to go out and dig into your own fiction project ... something that happened constantly to Unboxers during the live version.

As such, we've arranged this book into what feels like the three most logical chunks:

SECTION 1: The Campaign, which follows the whys and whats that preceded *Fiction Unboxed:* how we got the idea to write a book live, how we shaped that idea, how we prepared, how we launched our successful crowdfunding campaign, and what we learned.

SECTION 2: *Fiction Unboxed*, which chronicles the events of June 1-30 of 2014, when we came up with our book's idea from scratch, then wrote (and published) it in full. In order to give you the full scoop here, we can't avoid spoilers. **So if you think you'd like to read the book in question — a young adult steampunk novel called** *The Dream Engine* — **without spoilers, you may want to do so BEFORE reading this one.**

SECTION 3: Building a World Together, which tells the story after the story: the rallying of a small group of insiders at our World Builder Summit just two months after the live project wrapped, each dedicated to writing "canon" books in the shared world that would intertwine with and complement our core series. The world we'd created was (and remains) open for anyone to write and sell books in — without asking permission, without paying us a cent or giving us copyright — and the Summit heralded that "open source fiction" kickoff with a bang.

Each chapter throughout the book concludes with a few takeaways and "action steps." We went back and forth on including these, waffling between offering an overt list detailing what you should've learned versus burying those points in the narrative. In the end, we decided you shouldn't have to dig for what we consider to be this book's prime takeaways. Those end-of-chapter sections are "the least you need to know" if you otherwise breeze through some sections.

Before we delve in, we'd like to say something about the action steps in particular. You'll be tempted to ignore them. Please don't. One of the magic things that happened during the live project was the activity in our forums and endless e-mails from writers declaring, "Holy crap, I got inspired from watching you guys and ended up writing my way past a huge block I've had forever!"

We want that to happen for you. *Fiction Unboxed* was designed as a kind of virtual apprenticeship, and apprenticeships aren't passive.

You watch ... but then you do.

We hope this book will inspire you to new heights, and enhance the magic of writing.

And then we hope you'll *get out there and do.*

Ladies and Gentlemen, Welcome to the Greatest Writing Show on Earth!

HURRY, HURRY ... STEP RIGHT UP!

Gather 'round, my writer friends. I have a story to tell, the likes of which you've never heard.

So you say that writing can be a mysterious and frustrating game? That you sometimes wonder how other authors get their ideas, and how they struggle through a novel's trickiest parts? You say you're occasionally — perhaps often — plagued by doubt as you tell your tale? That you wonder if you're good enough, if your plot twists enough, if your characters grow enough from a story's start to finish? That you're not sure if your work should teach a lesson — or if so, whether that lesson will come off as pompous and heavy-handed? And most of all, do I hear you declaring that the muse is fickle — that sometimes words come too slowly, or refuse to come at all?

I know what you mean, fellow writer. I've walked that road, and know just how lonely it can be.

Because, friend, I've been there. In 1999, I started writing my first novel ... but I didn't finish it until 2011. It took me that long — with a lot of life in between — to turn my rambling tale into something that others might want to read. Stephen King once compared the process of writing a novel to crossing the ocean in a bathtub, and I could relate. When you're halfway through your journey and unsure where you are, sometimes all you can do is to keep going, hoping that everything will work out.

Writing can be hard, like building an engine is hard. But at least in the field of engine-building there are courses and apprenticeships. At least there are people out there who will show you, bolt by bolt, how it's done. But that's not true with writing. There are some great books out there on the craft, and in the twelve-year span between beginning my first novel and finishing it, I read a lot of them. But reading is never the same as seeing, and studying lessons is not the same as an apprenticeship at an expert's side, observing their every move. And yet, try as I did during those dozen years, I couldn't find any successful writers willing to let me stand behind them, taking notes, as they penned their masterpieces.

And so I did what most writers do.

I winged it.

I guessed.

I hoped.

Eventually, I more or less figured it out. And hey ... it only took twelve years.

That's how it's always been ... or at least, how it *used* to be.

Friend, if this sounds familiar — if you've traveled that long and lonely road, without balm in hand to soothe your tired writer's feet — I'd like to invite you to step closer, settle in, and listen. Because I've got a story to tell you about two crazy young writers who, once upon a time, decided to do what nobody else had done before: they decided to write a novel live in thirty days — starting from nothing — while an audience played fly on the wall to every detail of their process.

On the first day, with a ticking clock and all eyes on them, these two daredevils started with nothing at all: no characters, no world or setting, no plot ... not even a genre to write in.

And then, over the course of the coming month, with the world's eyes upon them, they conceived, brainstormed, outlined, wrote, edited, polished, proofread, compiled, and published their tale. The audience watched as they shared their new, raw words every day — often before the other half of the duo had even read them. Watchers peeked over the writers' shoulders, seeing every one of their story meetings and reading all their correspondence — through good times and bad, through ideas that fell flat and discussions full of "Eureka!" moments. The audience saw the birth of the book's protagonist, then watched her come to life on a commissioned book cover. And on the thirtieth day, every one of those people had the completed hundred thousand-word book in hand.

At the end, those observers had *seen how it was done*, start to finish, bolt by bolt — thanks to two daredevils who decided to walk a scribe's tightrope with no net. Two thrill-seekers who'd gone into their crazy experiment knowing they might fail ... but who thrived instead, and lived to tell the tale.

So, friend, let me ask you again: Do you suffer from storyline insecurity? Writer's block? Character maladies and malnourished themes? Does your plot twist and turn like a trick hip? Is your mood down, your dander up? Are you plagued by shady foreshadowing and drooping drama — a scribe's malady that no elixir can cure?

Well then step right up, ladies and gentlemen, and I'll tell you a tale to fix what ails you. A yarn to sow your garden with enough story seeds that you'll never go hungry again. It'll return the zip to your zazzle and strip the perspiration from your inspiration!

You're about to read the story of the Greatest Writing Show on Earth: that of *Fiction Unboxed* and the word-tallying, podcast-rallying, electrifying, mesmerizing, Dave-doubt-defying *Dream Engine!*

Come one, come all, and take your seats around the stage. The show's about to start!

PART ONE: THE CAMPAIGN

CHAPTER ONE:
The Idea

DURING THE LEAD-UP TO *Fiction Unboxed's* thirty-day live performance (a rather tense bit of improv authorship that birthed my favorite of our books so far: a young adult steampunk novel called *The Dream Engine*), Sean and I wrote a script for a promotional video that went, in part, like this:

> I'm Johnny B. Truant. In 1999, I wrote my first novel. In 2012, I wrote my second. Then, in 2013, I met my writing partner, Sean Platt, and together we wrote and published the equivalent of one and a half times the entire Harry Potter series.

Something tells me I might never forget that little bit of monologue, despite the initial difficulty I had in memorizing it for the shoot. It so perfectly sums up the magic that leapt into my life soon after I met Sean and Dave and we started recording the *Self-Publishing Podcast*. I had slaved and slaved over my "coming of age, with dick jokes" novel, *The Bialy Pimps*, but after spending a few months with Sean and Dave and seeing how they worked up close, something clicked. I began to realize something I'd never managed to realize before: *Telling stories, in and of itself, is easy. It's only getting them out that can be hard.*

I'd been writing all my life. I wrote one-pagers in this big yellow kids' book called *My Book About Me*. I wrote accidentally hilarious letters to my grandmother before I knew how to properly use a period or comma. I wrote a Dave Barry-esque column for my high school newspaper, full of reasons why I, at age fifteen, knew better than I know today. I worked as a freelance copywriter. I wrote around a hundred feature-length stories for prominent magazines, each tops in their fields.

I knew *how to write* just fine. What I didn't know (I thought) was *how to tell a story.*

What I learned by watching Sean and Dave churn out a book a week through their Collective Inkwell imprint (now one of six imprints under our parent company, Sterling & Stone) was that storytelling isn't difficult at all, because we've been hearing stories all our lives.

Think about that for a second.

If you're like most people, you heard your first story before you could understand it. Almost anyone who will ever see these words grew up reading books, watching narratives unfold on TV and the big screen, and hearing tales spun by folksy old grandparents while rocking in chairs. We *know* story. And if you're like I was, you also *know writing.*

So when writers flounder, what's the problem? And perhaps more importantly, what's the solution?

Well, it's not to read more books about how to write. I tried that in spades. It's also not to attend workshops or get critiques from other writers. It's not to study grammar. Those things are great and necessary and advisable and wise, but they're not the solution to floundering — not unless you want to take the long way around, as I did between 1999 and 2011.

Skills should be practiced and honed, and you'll always be a better writer tomorrow if you practice your craft today. But for most writers, the fatal problem — the one that keeps them from finishing novels or makes writing more difficult than it needs to be — isn't with their skills. It's with their perceptions, methods, confidence, and sense of internal resistance.

The many writing books I've absorbed over the years taught me a lot. And similarly, when we at the podcast wrote our own "writing and publishing book," *Write. Publish. Repeat: The No-Luck-Required Guide to Self-Publishing Success* in 2013, readers e-mailed in droves to tell us that *it* taught *them* a lot, too. But even after finishing the tome, people had the same question for us that I'd had for other authors throughout those twelve long years:

Okay, I understand what I need to do. But how do I do it?

For a few weeks, that question perplexed us. Wasn't "understanding what I need to do" the same as "understanding how to do it"? It's not, and this book is the story of how we tried to answer the latter question rather than the former.

Because again, *you already know how to tell a story*, if you can get out of your own way enough to see it. And there's also an excellent chance, if you're reading this, that *you already know how to write.*

What's left is learning the alchemy required to combine those two things, and strengthen a few less-tangible skills: confidence, the strength to murder resistance, a sense that your struggles aren't wrong or unusual, and writer's best practices. What's left is to study, like an apprentice, at the shoulder of a master.

I can't call myself a "master" with a straight face, and Sean and Dave are even less willing. But we *have* published millions upon millions of fiction words loved by our fans.

And in 2013, after struggling to write a single novel over the course of a dozen years, I *did* find a way to publish many well-reviewed books, totaling over 1.5 million words, in 2013 alone.

Before we had the idea to do the live *Fiction Unboxed* experiment in June of 2014, we considered writing a book that we hoped would help readers of *Write. Publish. Repeat.* understand our process.

But in an apprenticeship, you don't *explain* your process. You *show* it.

Here's how it all began.

We Only Tell Stories. Sorta.

We didn't set out to be nonfiction authors. Really, we didn't.

I met Sean online because we both wrote for a popular website called Copyblogger. Copyblogger is tops in its field, but not a haven for story-spinners. It's more about marketing, like how to make your business better and attract more leads. And yes, the site has plenty of writing advice, but it's usually copywriting stuff: how to write a lede that draws people in and fuels their desire to read more. How to keep them on the page by promising open loops that won't be closed until later. How to write an effective call to action as your closing, urge a reader to buy, or perhaps sign up for your offer or newsletter.

Sean has a natural love of movies, books, and stories in general, but he segued sideways into copywriting because he's terminally infected with the entrepreneurism gene and did quite well as a scribe for hire. I'd been writing all my life and had always wanted to pen novels, but in 2008, when I started online, there was still no way to make a living as a fiction writer unless you got lucky and hit the right literary agent with the ideal (and appropriately marketable) novel at the perfect time. So I, too, asked myself how I could make money with words. Copyblogger had many of the answers.

What I didn't realize at the time was that Sean (who I knew in the way F-List, "Internet famous" people know one another) was already working with David Wright — an artist who fit the "marketing and copy for hire" mold as well as a duck fits in a keyhole. If Sean and I wanted to be storytellers and diverted into marketing reluctantly, Dave must have done so kicking and screaming.

So there we were: three guys who wanted to be creatives, stuck doing what my artist father affectionately called "whoring our talents." Sean and I were good at marketing, but marketing, in and of itself, was never our goal. We wanted to tell tales. We wanted to build worlds, but our families needed to eat. And there was no feasible way, in 2008, to build a sensible business around fiction.

Although I had a huge head start in fiction (a 150,000-word boondoggle of a manuscript I'd sent to agents and subsequently given up on), Sean and Dave took their shot at selling their creative work first. Before the Kindle hit the market, they wanted it badly enough to try selling small print-on-demand "Wee Books." Sean's never told me how well they sold, but I'm thinking it must have been enough money to supersize a Happy Meal, if they were willing to share.

Sean and Dave published serialized fiction on their Collective Inkwell blog, posting new chapters of their first fiction together, *Available Darkness*, one chapter per week. Readers loved it, but the audience was relatively small and difficult to grow.

Then came the Kindle and a transformation of the Inkwell. Overnight, it went from a site where Sean and Dave hung their shingle, hoping for copy and design jobs, to the tiny publishing house responsible for the first "season" of their cult hit serial *Yesterday's Gone*.

Yesterday's Gone eventually exploded in popularity, but it suffered the same slow start as any new series. And while it was still limping along and earning pennies, Sean decided to launch his first information product: a high-value copywriting course called *Sales Letter Shortcut*. This was Sean's sliding door moment, an axis upon which everything to follow might be entirely different, and he recalls feeling like he had to make a choice: Do I want to sell nonfiction courses? Or do I want to put my stakes in the sand and declare to the universe that I am a fiction writer?

Sales Letter Shortcut was on the market for exactly one day. The second morning, Sean closed it down and refunded everyone who'd bought it. *That's* how badly he wanted to be a fiction writer.

While Sean was facing his own fork in the road, I was doing the same. I'd created a rather popular blog with a five-digit following, and as Sean was choosing art over relatively easy profit (surely with Dave shoving from behind), I found myself facing one suspiciously loaded choice after another. Something creative I'd written would take off while a "sure thing" moneymaker would somehow fail. I was less willing to leap before looking than Sean, so I needed a push. My nonfiction profits were drying, so when I interviewed Sean about his "crazy experiments in fiction writing," it was simple enough to start dabbling myself.

I'm a compulsive type when it comes to interests and dreams, and Sean and Dave's quickly growing fiction success had rekindled that old spark inside me — the spark of writing fiction for a living that I'd thought was dead and buried forever. Passion fueled me and made me forget about money — a good thing, because for nearly a year there was barely more than a dime at a time. And so while my wife, Robin, watched in horror, I diverted to full-time fiction writing in mere months, leaving our bank dry enough to cry.

I'll fast-forward at this point, because you've already heard this story if you read *Write. Publish. Repeat.* or listen to our podcast. Here's the quick version: I wrote the six-book *Fat Vampire* saga, which gave my fiction career the jumpstart it needed. Sean and I wrote a ton of books in several genres at our new imprint, Realm & Sands, while Sean and Dave continued to turn the crank on horrors and nightmares at Collective Inkwell. Little by little, life — and our bank accounts — improved. We were full-time fiction authors, living our dreams.

But behind all that fiction was the *Self-Publishing Podcast* we'd started together — a podcast with an audience of writers, which helped to advance our author platforms and promote our novels and serials. It was, in other words, a *nonfiction* audience that was accidentally instrumental in bringing us together, making us stronger, and helping to craft our careers as they exist today. *SPP* was a conduit through which we reached hybrid fans — people who wanted to know how we operated our publishing businesses (now one big business under Sterling & Stone) as authorpreneurs, but who also read and loved our flights of fancy.

We'd always wanted to be fiction authors ... but our fiction business had, as its backbone and catalyst, a huge nonfiction entity. We were where we were because of the *Self-Publishing Podcast*, the brain trust it had fostered, the friendships it had forged, and the audience it had built.

I've said many times on the show, "If it weren't for *SPP*, I wouldn't be an author today." And it's true.

Yes, we wanted to be fiction authors. But we found that we also love the nonfiction aspects of what we do. Recording the podcasts (we have another called *Better Off Undead*, but you should avoid that one at all costs) are the highlights of our week. We love interacting with our listeners. We love it when writers e-mail us — and this happens many times each week — to tell us that *SPP* got them moving, gave them confidence, allowed them to finally write and publish the thing they'd been working on for years. A friend of mine once said, "If you don't get regular thanks in your job, I don't think you should do that job anymore." And I agree, with all my heart.

So there we were: fiction writers with a nonfiction core. Storytellers with students. Spinners of yarn who, no matter how we sliced it, had an obligation (a *delightful* obligation) to speak, in real-world terms, about what it was we did all day and how we'd built and sustained full-time careers as authors.

After a year of doing the *Self-Publishing Podcast* every week, we decided to condense all we knew about independent writing and publishing into a single volume — something we wanted to be a bible of self-publishing. Our concession to nonfiction: we'd write the book, then move on with more stories.

But *Write. Publish. Repeat.* had other plans for us. Its launch was explosive, hitting and hanging out in the Amazon Top 100. It sells better in print and audiobook than anything we've published so far, by orders of magnitude. We're still flooded with great reviews, long e-mails of thanks, and flattering mentions alongside the names of other great authors who helped to shape our lives and style.

But as the first wave died down, we looked at each other and said, "That was fun. Now let's get back to telling stories."

Yet those e-mails of thanks harbored more than appreciation, and that something pulled us back into nonfiction as surely as Michael Corleone in *The Godfather Part III.*

It was a question.

Productivity vs. Process

As with this book, *Write. Publish. Repeat.* was written primarily by Sean and me, with Dave contributing here and there. When Sean and I write together, we're like a wonder-filled factory. We plow through words in mountainous piles, in part because we don't believe in writer's block. Each project has a deadline, and we seldom miss one. This is a *business*, dammit, even though it's a business founded (and filled with) magic. In business, you're not allowed to miss deadlines or go over budget.

The budget for *Write. Publish. Repeat.* was originally fifty thousand words. We quickly realized it would require sixty thousand, and reluctantly extended the deadline accordingly. But as I wrote, I kept sheepishly reporting to Sean: "It's going to take 75K." "Man, I think this may top 100K." "Sorry, dude, but it looks more like 120K."

Even after spilling almost two and a half times our original budget into the book, we had to axe an entire productivity section from the end of the outline. We simply didn't have time to write another huge swatch of words on this already over-budget project, and knew we'd imposed on our readers' time enough already. It was time to call it quits. We mentioned the missing section at the end and promised to hit it later, in a follow-up book. It seemed that another bit of nonfiction had landed on our "eventual" plate.

The book dropped, and e-mails flooded. Many shared a central question: "When can we read the 'productivity' book you mentioned at the end?" Or really, once we read between the lines: "I understand what's in *Write. Publish. Repeat.* But still ... how the hell do you actually *do* it?"

People had loved all the nuts and bolts delivered in *WPR*, but the recurring inquiries were all about *how*, even after they knew *what*.

At first we took those questions to be about the omitted section; people wanted to hear our tips on how to be more productive, and that was all there was to it. But then we realized that wasn't it at all. People *thought* they wanted productivity, but that's a bit like thinking you want a drill when in fact all you really want is the hole. If all we did was tell people how to be more productive — how to budget time, how to eliminate distractions, how to get more words written in a given period of time — we wouldn't be answering their real question.

How do I write more good books, faster and with less difficulty?

That wasn't a productivity question. That was a *process* question.

I used to be a king of *productivity*. I could sit down and crank out two thousand words per hour, no problem. But what I found *over and over and over again* — as I tried to write a novel between 1999's *The Bialy Pimps* and 2011's *Fat Vampire* — was that all of my stories went nowhere. I'd create these wonderful scenes, then have no idea where to take them. I didn't know what came next or what should have come before, to prep and foreshadow a reader. I had no idea how to budget my effort, how much to do with each stage of my draft, how to track loose ends and embed reader-delighting callbacks later into the manuscript. I didn't know how to "listen to what the story was trying to tell me" and follow threads on faith. I didn't understand how much to plan in advance (I thought outlining was anathema to creativity and had no clue about the "anti-outlining" preproduction process Sean and I use today) or how to follow any preplanned structure while still allowing for deviations ... or how much to deviate if so. Other than what I could glean from books (which were sterile by nature; no writer wants to show you his or her true guts), I didn't know how successful writers moved from book's start to book's end. I didn't get what they changed during edits, how they polished and salted mentions of important events throughout their works, how they knew when it was ready for publication, how much feedback to get, or any of the stuff that actually mattered.

It wasn't that I wasn't *capable* of doing any of that work. It was that I didn't know what to do. I didn't know that most of my struggles were typical. Did a confused character mean my failure as a writer, or was it a natural part of the process? Did writers routinely make messes before crafting beautiful stories, or was their work clean in scope (albeit rough in execution) the first time through?

If, in the early 2000s, someone had given me productivity tips, they wouldn't have helped me at all. I was plenty productive. I needed to understand *process*, and know that I wasn't alone in my struggles. I needed to know that if I was smart and persistent, those knots could work themselves out.

So we shifted our thinking. People thought they wanted productivity tips, but what they really wanted was to understand our process — the process that allows us to pump out twenty-five thousand words or more of publishable content, *per week*.

Learning a better process will help you achieve superior results and smile more along the way. Only then should you turn to productivity ... so you do what you're currently doing faster and more efficiently.

But Screw That.

No matter how we split hairs over productivity versus process, we still weren't nonfiction guys and didn't want to write a follow-up to *Write. Publish. Repeat.* anytime soon. The growth of *WPR* from a two-week book to a six-week book (I ended up going over it a final time after Sean was finished, which wasn't originally part of the plan) had annihilated our production calendar and forced us to bump two fiction projects we'd been dying to write — one a Harry Potter-age novel that's been bumped twice more this year and still isn't finished. WPR had been great, but it was time to count our dead (or delayed, I suppose) and move on.

Collective Inkwell had caught my attention with their habit of turning out a serial-length "episode" every single week. When I joined Sean and Dave on the podcast, I thought that feat was superhuman, and commented on the insanity often. But I learned more "process stuff" myself and grew increasingly inspired. I began to produce even faster. I wrote *Fat Vampire* and *Fat Vampire 2* in a month each, then found that speed more than doubled when I teamed with Sean for our first two projects: a surprisingly deep fantasy epic mash-up called *Unicorn Western* and a political, hard sci-fi serial called *The Beam*.

Sean and I are both incurably ADD in nature, unable to choose between A and B and always tending to select the unspoken third option: *both*. Our problem is that we think everything is awesome. Our story meetings are like tossing tennis balls to puppies. We're always bouncing around, saying how amazing everything is.

In the year before writing *WPR*, Sean had pitched me six new projects to accompany our preexisting half-dozen: three ideas for serials and three ideas for what we thought of as "written sitcoms." The plan was to pick one from each pile, then write a full "season" of both — one serial and one comedy. But true to form, we decided that all our concepts were too awesome to ignore and wrote pilots for all six. And so as *WPR* rolled toward publication, and then as it hit big, Sean and I were focused on finishing the full seasons of all those projects.

We had no room for a "process" book, or any interest in shoving one in. Even our current workload meant putting in a bunch of ten-thousand-word days just inches from Christmas. But as grueling as that might sound to some people, *it was also a ridiculous amount of fun.*

That notion seeped heavily into the seed of an idea that bloomed into *Fiction Unboxed*: that writing fiction should always be fun. We worked our faces off at the end of 2013, but I've never laughed more or harder. And it's not because we write such cheery material. Some of our books harbor laughs, but many are dead serious, disturbing, violent, or uncomfortable. There are moments that make readers cry, and always moments that make readers think. But regardless of a story's content, writing them can be fun. And at least for Sean and me, they always are.

As e-mails asking for productivity and process continued to pour in, we thought a lot about fun. How can we produce so much? Because we love what we're doing as much as we do, we're willing to put in the hours. Time feels weightless. The more story meetings we have, the more excited we get about each of our stories. When I hit a scintillating scene, our cell phones erupt in a flurry of excited texts. Our energy stays high, and we *want to work.* It's not always that way for us, but we began to ponder why. What makes for a slow, sluggish writing day? Usually for us, it meant being out of flow, such as when we returned from a week away from the page.

Little by little, we began building mental file folders dedicated to explaining why our process works as well as it does. As 2013 wound down and Sean and I completed "product funnels" for each of our stories (which usually meant finishing a series or the first "season" of a serial), we began to outline our process book without even meaning to.

Sean writes rough "story beats" for a new project. We have a meeting to discuss those beats, and the meeting is fun. I get excited. That makes the writing fun. The harder we work, the more fun we have. The only hard times are when our flow breaks ... and the more we write, the better our flow becomes.

Our thoughts on process weren't remotely coherent as we finished all that fiction, but the seed had been planted. We don't believe in formulas, but there *was* a formula to what we did nonetheless, and I think both our minds had begun to scratch at that bottomless itch.

What was the secret?

Why didn't we ever get writer's block?

Why did we see the *concept* of writer's block as so incredibly absurd?

People always ask writers where they get their ideas, so why did it feel like we had more ideas than we'd ever manage to tap? We'd taken something Dave mentioned in jest as a "stupid idea" and turned it into what readers tell us is an unforgettable story. Over and over, we'd stumbled across random thoughts, then turned them into plot points within our in-progress stories as if they'd been born there. What was it about our process — our formula that wasn't a formula — that made it so simple to turn almost *any* idea into gold?

We knew that there were no formulas, per se — that anyone who wants to do something well needs to find her own way, and that talk of "formula" is merely a manipulative technique used to trick suckers with dreams of quick fixes into spending dollars on bullshit.

So you can imagine how unhappy I was when Sean sent me an entirely inappropriate text ... even if that inappropriate text planted the seeds for the *Fiction Unboxed* project.

A Pair of Assholes

It's November of 2013, late for me, maybe ten at night, when I get a text from Sean that goes something like this:

> Dude. Hear me out. But what do you think of *The Fiction Formula* as a name for our book?

I stared at my iPhone. The book in question was the one that became *Write. Publish. Repeat.* (a much better name suggested by a podcast listener named Shannon Morgan), and Sean was sending me this text just weeks before publication. The book already had a name. And a cover, with said name on it. We'd referred to it over and over again on our website, in e-mails, and on the podcast itself.

But what was worse, I thought as I stared at my screen with a scalp on fire, was that we didn't *believe* in formulas. We'd said it repeatedly on our podcasts, in blog posts, and to anyone who would listen: "There is no formula. If anyone tells you there's a formula, they're about to ask you for $97."

That's a recurring joke on our show, because all infomercial products (99 percent of which Dave feels are evil) seem to have prices that end in sevens. Unlike Dave, Sean and I have *paid* $97 for info products without being scammed or duped, and feel they were of excellent value, but we both felt the universe nudging us away from instruction and toward fiction. We'd grudgingly sell nonfiction if people wanted it, and we could deliver great value, but there was no damned way I would ever allow myself to be associated with a "formula."

I texted back:

Are you kidding? Tell me you're kidding.

I didn't wait for Sean's response. I wrote one or two more long-winded texts detailing our firm stance against formulas, our oft-stated opinions that those who sold formulas were consummate bullshitters, and my general shock that he'd even *consider* pitching me such a stupid idea.

Then I waited for a response that never came.

This went on for a good thirty seconds before I decided that Sean was 1) drunk, 2) being unduly influenced by the asshole I knew he was having dinner with, and 3) transforming into an asshole himself. I kept waiting for a response, then finally decided that 4) Sean was pissed at me for my ranting and that we were in trouble.

As it turned out, Sean's phone was glitchy that night, and he didn't call me until the next day because he hadn't seen my texts. By then I'd calmed down, but still wondered what the hell was wrong with him. I knew the asshole he was having dinner with and rather like him despite his admitted assholishness, but this formula crap was too much.

SEAN PLATT & JOHNNY B. TRUANT

Sean heard me out, then gave his reply. What's so annoying about Sean is that I usually agree with him even when I don't want to. There were some seriously excellent points that had been made during this dinner between two assholes, and I had to admit it. Sean is a business genius, and the other asshole happened to be a #1 *New York Times* best-selling author and a general Gandalf of marketing who's sold more than five million books. Neither has a scammy personality, and Sean, at least, knew the *Self-Publishing Podcast* and Sterling & Stone brands. He knew how I'd react, but had thought it worthy of mentioning anyway.

"We'll have to position it just right, and have a section at the front that explains, despite the title, that there is no formula," he said. "The book itself won't change — just the title and that introduction. It's a headline, nothing more."

The phrase "It's a headline" is shorthand between us, so I got what he was saying right away. We both came out of copywriting, and understand that a headline's purpose is the same as a fisherman's lure. You want to draw a potential reader in with something interesting, then show them your offer. A headline is a flashing marquee. It's a targeted advertisement. It's one of those big air-dancer things, or the thousand balloons a car dealer ties to antennae.

"We'll look like scammers," I said. "We'll look like hypocrites to our audience, promising a formula — if only in the title."

But then Sean enumerated the points: There'd never been a book quite like *Write. Publish. Repeat* that explains how fiction writers in particular can build a sensible marketing plan around a body of work. There were plenty of books like that for nonfiction writers — books that explained the use of nonfiction work as lead generators, designed to pull readers into other books or paid services — but not for novelists. We'd created a way of commoditizing fiction that no one else had, and yet our title did nothing to attract the readers who'd be most interested in it. There was no formula ... but given that nobody really talked about fiction marketing and fiction product funnels quite like we had, the truth said it was closer to a formula than anything before it. Besides, Sean argued, there's nothing sleazy about *hooking* people with the idea of a formula. What's sleazy is promising an instant and infallible money machine, and *WPR*, under any title, promised the opposite. The first 20 percent is all about how difficult it is to build a career as a fiction writer, and encourages readers to quit yesterday if they're expecting instant riches.

We tossed the idea around, with me growing calmer. *The Fiction Formula* was a horrid title to us, but there was no question it would reach a wider audience than the more nebulously titled *Write. Publish. Repeat.* We didn't want to trick anyone and *definitely* didn't want to overpromise, but we did want the book to end up in the right hands. Putting a fiction formula in the headline was a surefire way to make sure fiction writers who struggled with marketing and selling would at least give it a glance.

We seriously considered the idea for one long day, but ultimately decided it was too far off-brand and would alienate more people in our audience than it would please. And that's one of our core tenants: Pleasing our current fans and readers will always be more important to us than attracting new ones. If we called our first how-to book *The Fiction Formula*, it could very well cripple the *Self-Publishing Podcast* community. It might net us more book sales, yes. But it would also mar our reputations, and we rather liked them as they were.

But like a persistent housefly, the idea wouldn't leave us alone. As *Write. Publish. Repeat.* rolled toward publication under its original name, we talked about writing a Fiction Formula manifesto, almost tongue in cheek, and putting it up for sale cheap (or ideally free) as a lead generator to steer people toward *WPR*. We talked about titling our second nonfiction book *The Fiction Formula*, but handling all the preliminary discussion by making it clear that the idea of a formula was a joke. We even thought about adding a parenthetical to the title in order to keep our noses clean: *The Fiction Formula (There Is No Formula)*.

None of those ideas bore fruit, but in early 2014 we began to think a bit outside the book. Maybe we didn't need to write a follow-up to *WPR* — at least, not yet. Maybe we could do something else. Something visual. Something experiential. Something huge, and raw, and real, and brave.

We harkened back to 2013's flood of requests for a process book detailing what we do to produce a novel from scratch, and the two ideas ran to hug each other like chocolate greeting peanut butter. It hit us hard: what those people had been asking for was a formula — a *fiction formula* – just like Asshole #1 had said.

"I know we can't write out some kind of formula," Sean said, rubbing his chin. "But what if we *show* it instead?"

I've known Sean long enough now that I can usually pre-guess what he's going to say. The trick isn't to understand his intentions and realize that although what he's saying sounds crazy, it actually isn't. The trick is to understand that it's *thoroughly batshit*, and that Sean simply doesn't care.

"You want to write a novel in front of a live audience because of that whole fiction formula thing, don't you?" I said.

Sean grinned.

APPLY IT! This Chapter's Takeaways and Action Steps

Here's the least you need to know from this chapter:

- Listen to your audience. If you do, they will tell you ways to better serve them.
- But as you do, understand that people don't always understand what they really want. Our tribe asked for *productivity*, but what they truly wanted was *process*.
- Search for intersections between *what your readers want most* and *where you want to take your career.* Find the overlaps and pursue *those* projects so you can maximally benefit — both creatively and professionally.

And here's something you can do **RIGHT NOW** to apply this chapter's lessons:

- Make a list of everything you believe your audience (or ideal audience) would like from you. Then make a list of the projects you want to write most. Look for intersections. (HINT: They may take some time to find, so keep at it.)

CHAPTER TWO:
The Pitch

So THAT'S HOW IT HAPPENED, huh? That's how we decided to do *Fiction Unboxed*?

Um, no.

You guys don't know Sean. If you listen to our podcast, you may *think* you know how he is, but you don't. On air, you get 10 percent of Sean's actual enthusiasm. Off the air, he has at least a thousand new ideas per hour, and each one excites him. Imagine a Labrador retriever who loves chasing balls, then imagine throwing that Lab into one of those ball pits kids play in at Chuck E. Cheese's. That's Sean.

His wacko idea to write a book live in front of an audience was interesting, but it's not like it felt groundbreaking at the time, and I had no idea it would develop into our biggest and most creatively satisfying endeavor to date.

You've gotta understand — in the time we've worked together, Sean has pitched Dave and me on the "very real" possibilities of a traditional book contract with a six-figure advance, a movie deal with a William Morris agent, a Netflix series, a partnership with a huge media website with a brand name and an enormous budget, and much more. Cool ideas and excellent prospects are par for the course. Most of these things don't work out, or require more time to simmer than any of us expect.

Sean's enthusiasm is contagious, and the ups and downs of following it are exhausting. While Dave remains cynical of everything (Dave still isn't convinced the sun will come out tomorrow), I always get sucked right in. Time and time again, I've been excited about something only to watch it fall flat. But like a good Labrador retriever, shortfalls don't faze Sean. He's back up a minute later, panting, "Can we do it again? Can we? Can we? Huh? Huh?"

So sure, the idea of writing a book live sounded groundbreaking and exciting, but so does everything Sean pitches. I got excited for a few minutes then returned my attention to our current project — the one that hadn't even launched before my partner was running off and doing flips over something that was, at its core, completely impractical.

Because sure, writing a book live would show *SPP* and *WPR* fans the process they'd been clamoring to see. And sure, it would allow us to handle the persnickety "productivity" question without having to write another nonfiction book. But Sean wasn't seeing that it would be a ton of work to unbox our process. We'd have to build a new website, do the nuts-and-bolts work required to make it members only, record all our story meetings in both audio and video (and surely get them transcribed), commit to blogging the entire process, schedule inevitable Q&A sessions with participants, rush our partners (our editor, cover illustrator, and proofreaders), rush *ourselves* (writing a rough draft in a month is easy for us, but opening and closing the entire preproduction, writing, editing, post-production, and publication process in thirty days? That's different), deal with customer service, tech support, inevitable administrative headaches, and every shred of minutiae. We'd also have to delay writing several projects on our already-packed production calendar. Because remember: We were full-time fiction authors still planting seeds in the growing phase of our careers. Writing books was *how we made our living*, so it's not like we could take a month or two off to handle every loose end that was sure to accompany a virtual apprenticeship.

Well, *maybe* we could. *If* we knew for sure that enough people would buy into whatever apprenticeship we offered for sale. Knowing that would help us plan. We'd be able to justify the time and money spent because we'd know we'd be compensated — enough to make up for the lost time and income.

But how could we possibly know that kind of thing in advance?

Kickstarted

There's a guy named ZC Bolger who's not only a listener of our podcast and a collaborator of one of our collaborators, but also the butt of most of our on-air jokes that don't center on Dave. ZC rolls with it, understanding that we bust his balls with affection, as we tell people to send any hate mail intended for us to his e-mail address and Twitter handle.

We also knew Zach as the Kickstarter guy.

If you're not familiar with Kickstarter, it's an online "crowdfunding" platform that allows people to propose ideas, then ask the world if they want to fund those ideas by pledging money, thus enabling the creator to render them into reality. There are a handful of similar platforms (IndieGoGo and GoFundMe come to mind), but Kickstarter, as of 2014, is the big dog. A creator sets a funding threshold on Kickstarter (say, $5,000), then typically has a month to acquire enough pledges to reach it. If the project reaches its minimum, it's considered funded. The backers are then charged for their pledge amounts, the creator receives the money, then she completes the promised project and rewards her supporters with whatever she promised during the campaign (typically the project to be created itself and variations thereof).

Sorry, Zach, but the truth is that when we first heard about the idea of using Kickstarter to fund the writing of a book, we thought it was kind of douchey. All three of us wrote our first novels while juggling day jobs, and we kind of figured it was a writer's due: deliver his time, do the hard work first, then receive payment later. Asking first felt like a plea for charity. "My dream is to write a book," it seemed to say. "How about you make my dream a reality for no reason other than I'm awesome and shouldn't have to do the hard work first?"

We expressed as much on the show, and one of our listeners left a comment that started massaging our minds. It basically said we had it all wrong. Kickstarter is a marketplace, not a call for donations, the listener wrote. Because all supporters are given "backer rewards" at a project's completion (with higher-pledging backers getting bigger rewards), it's most appropriate to see the transaction as a *purchase*, insisted our listener. In ZC's case, people were essentially *preordering his book* and maybe getting some neat bonuses as well. Given that Amazon didn't allow independent authors to offer preorders on their books until August of 2014, the idea of "preordering through Kickstarter" made even more sense. If Zach reached his funding goal, he'd write the book and deliver it to his backers. If he didn't, he wouldn't. It wasn't about charity. It was commerce, in advance.

Once that mental flip-flop occurred, the idea of crowdfunding "something" began to rattle around in our heads (mostly mine and Sean's; Dave still hates stuff). That com-

SEAN PLATT & JOHNNY B. TRUANT

ment changed our minds. Once it did, crowdfunding's true nature seemed so obvious that we wondered why we'd never seen it before. *It's a marketplace, not a charity drive.* We couldn't believe we'd missed it.

(In reality, the fact that the mental switcharoo was so hard to see came back to bite us in a very big way when we launched our own campaign, and we should probably have seen it coming. But more on that later.)

We never came around on the idea of Kickstarting individual books even before Amazon gave us the ability to do preorders, but the seed had been planted. We had an audience; our audience liked us and kept asking for more stuff that we couldn't afford to do (either in cash or in time spent away from our core business of writing fiction), but Kickstarter promised a simple way to determine our focus. We'd decide what amount of money would make a month's diversion from fiction writing worthwhile, set it as a Kickstarter minimum, and see what happened. If the project met the goal, we'd do it and consider ourselves compensated. If it fell short and failed to fund, we'd know there wasn't enough demand for that project, and we'd skip it. No harm, no foul.

But until Sean had his asshole dinner, the idea of Kickstarter was very much in the background. It was a "wouldn't it be cool, some day, if we could ever find an appropriate project, which we won't because we're fiction writers" sort of notion. We didn't want to Kickstart a book. It felt disingenuous, and flat-out unnecessary. We were writing books anyway, and made our money on the back end. Leaving flow to Kickstart another book or series felt like two jerks saying, "Hey, everyone ... how about you pay us now to write this thing we're going to write anyway?"

But now we had this perfect storm brewing. *WPR* readers and podcast listeners were clamoring to know how to write better books faster, and we'd already realized the only way to show them was to let them peek over our shoulders. Making that happen was a big deal and would take a lot of time ... but maybe Kickstarter (which we'd been intrigued by for a few months) was the answer. We could craft a Kickstarter campaign, set a reasonable minimum funding goal (one that, if we hit it, would account for the lost time and expense and make it worth our while), then let the campaign run for a month and see what happened. Hitting our goal would give us the compensation required to make the project worth doing. If we fell short, none of the backers would be charged a cent, we'd know the demand wasn't high enough to justify the doing, and we'd move on, continuing to write the novels we'd already planned to write.

In the spring of 2014, a few months after the successful launch of *Write. Publish. Repeat.* and as we were passing our production calendar's worst choke points, the balls in our heads (The Fiction Formula! Showing our process! Kickstarter!) began to bounce in a more logical order. An odd brew of magic descended — one that, like Sean's rabid enthusiasm, Dave and I have seen again and again.

Sean is excitable, yes. But he's also a motherfucking genius. As concepts gelled three things started to happen:

First, the "crazy idea" moved from the kind of unbridled giddiness that accompanies all of Sean's early notions into a more mature breed of giddiness — one that feels more like *possibility*.

Second, Dave started to freak out. He said things like, "You're not seriously thinking of letting people *watch you write*, are you? You aren't really going to *let people read your first drafts and watch you screw things up before getting them right,* are you?"

And third, I stepped into that same uncertainty, thrilled. On most things, Sean and I are *sympatico,* and the quirk of being excited by an insane challenge is certainly one of them. *Yes,* I was going to let people watch me write. *Yes,* I was willing to let people read my raw first draft and watch me screw up. The same things that frightened Dave crackled my brain like a campfire. I couldn't wait to get started.

After bowing out of the spotlight and opting for a supporting role in the project, Dave asked Sean and me in one of our meetings, "Doesn't the idea of writing a book in front of an audience scare you?"

I said, "It *absolutely* scares me. But I can't wait to do it anyway."

South By Southwest

In 2009, my friend Charlie Gilkey badgered me until I finally agreed to attend the South by Southwest interactive conference in Austin, Texas. I had an Internet-based business, he argued in his slight Southern drawl, and that meant I *had* to be at South by Southwest — something he always abbreviates as "South by" — for networking reasons, and also to get out and meet folks I only knew virtually.

I'll forever be grateful to Charlie for that push, because like so many tiny events, it was a sliding door moment that changed everything. I fell in love with Austin immediately, and seeing all my online friends was a kick. I slept on a couch at my friends Pace and Kyeli's house (P&K are a lesbian couple who, I was honored to learn, had never before had "a strange Internet man" stay over before me) and spent a week hanging out.

I returned in 2010, which seemed more subdued. The next year was even quieter for some reason, and 2012, which was the first year I dragged Sean along, was trending toward crickets for my own little group. That year, it was mainly me, Sean, Pace, and Kyeli. Our group was trending away from SXSW, and I wasn't sure why.

Still, that 2012 visit (which wouldn't have happened if I hadn't dragged Sean there; thanks, Charlie, for the nudge) was enough to prompt Sean to pack his family and move to Austin six months later — which, by the way, is the reason I'll hopefully be moving there in 2015. So when I returned to Austin for my annual pilgrimage in 2013, it was natural to stay with Sean given that Pace and Kyeli had moved to Portland. And good thing, because everyone else in my usual group had stopped going to SXSW all at once. Nobody sent me the memo. The dearth of activity meant there was little to do but mastermind with Sean ... but as with most things, that, too, seemed to happen for a reason.

Sean and I spent SXSW 2013 far from downtown: just me and the Platts, hanging out in a rotating background of Sean's apartment, the business center downstairs, a charming carry-out owned by a soft-spoken man named Nev, Starbucks, and the winding walking trail in between. It was perfect. Because while I missed my usual Austin buddies, Sean and I had a mountain of business to climb.

If you aren't living your dream job, you might think that business is a dirty word, but that's far from the case for us. We plotted and strategized from first light to midnight. We talked at Starbucks. We talked on the walking trail. We talked in the car on the way to a Lockhart barbecue joint called Smitty's, at Best Buy, in the business center, and in front of

Nev's coffee carafes, which Nev insisted on brewing fresh for us every time. Later, Nev told Sean's wife, Cindy, "I have never seen two people talk so much."

What had been a mere glimmer of a "someday/maybe" idea became tangible during my time in Austin. It became exciting. We couldn't stop hammering nails of promise into the details. "Does this scare you?" we kept asking each other. "Fuck yeah, let's do it!" was our usual response.

We untangled logistics. We planned the Kickstarter rewards. Time and again, we asked ourselves how to position the project. Recalling our initial douche-chills about the platform and its default feel of "begging for money," we wanted to pack our campaign with so much value that nobody could possibly complain. We wanted crazy cool to seep from its pores. We wanted more awesomeness in *Fiction Unboxed* (which finally had a name without formula in it, a concept now twice defeated) than grease on the butcher paper at Smitty's.

As we worked ("work" no longer being a four-letter word in either of our lives), the prospect of writing a book live became increasingly exciting. That was its own lesson, the more we thought about it. What did our partnership stand for? More than anything, it stood for *fun*. The catalogue Sean and I have written together — mainly via our imprint Realm & Sands — sprints all over the genre map. We've written westerns, fantasy, political sci-fi, action/adventure, fiction as nonfiction, comedy, and more. But they've all been fun.

The more fun we're having, the better our stories are.

As with our fiction, the process of mapping out *Fiction Unboxed* was a giddy experience, and we felt the fun we had planning it spilling into the project itself. It felt like a nested story — as if we were writing the beats of our lives rather than the beats of a novel. In fiction, Sean gets ideas from everything; the entire time I was in Austin he was pulling cowboy names from Austin-area street signs to use as characters in our then-upcoming *Unicorn Apocalypse*. And so it was for *Fiction Unboxed*. We were characters in our own story — a story that, to our knowledge, had never been told.

We didn't discuss story ideas for use in whatever book we'd write during *Fiction Unboxed,* because the idea that "great ideas are everywhere" was part of what we were trying to prove. We wanted to start with a blank slate on June 1, but I wasn't worried. Two of Dave's throwaway comments on the podcast had birthed nearly a half million words of fiction between us. Nervousness faded into excitement, because our story was finding its shape. And as with any great story, uncertainty was part of the thrill. We never know what our characters might choose to do in the middle of a novel, and our endings often surprise us.

Why should we have had any idea how our live writing experiment would unfold? Why should the possibility of embarrassment or failure bother us? All great characters face the unknown. It's what makes them grow. *It's what makes a story worth telling.*

I left Austin energized, high on life.

Little did I know our story's characters of Johnny B. Truant and Sean Platt had already made their first big mistake.

Change the World With a Story

While I was still in Austin we scripted then shot a video for the top of our Kickstarter page, because more than anything else, videos sell people on the idea of backing campaigns. The process was obnoxious. We went to three different shops to buy audio equipment, then realized we couldn't even record that audio into my iPhone, our de facto camera. We recorded audio in one place and video in another, creating multiple takes for each bit of video, and screwing up repeatedly.

Remember how I said that work isn't a four-letter word for us? Well, somehow "shooting video" is.

But we got it done, burning half a day, and I left Austin with the task of cobbling our Kibbles 'n Bits of A/V into something workable.

At home, I realized how terrible our video was. It wasn't just bad, with terrible audio. It was unusable. Flat-out wrong.

At the time we wrote the script — late at night after a long day, attempting to buzz on Nev's coffee and mostly failing — it had seemed perfect. *Man, we nailed the value proposition! Man, we ended it with a strong call to action! And man, we really juiced up the middle with a compelling series of benefits to any potential backer!* But what our marketing-savvy minds had failed to grasp is that crowdfunding campaigns aren't successful because they hook and then convince a potential backer like a well-written long-form sales letter. Successful campaigns — ones that not only reach their funding goals but *over*fund to the tune of 150, 200, 300 percent — are based not on *getting* something, but *being part of* something.

To harken back to the idea of using crowdfunding as a preorder system, it's true that you can run a campaign, sell your stuff ahead of production, and walk away with a campaign that's just as successful as a normal launch would have been — albeit one conducted with payment beforehand rather than afterward. But if you do that, you have to aim low. You'll be supplying most of the audience yourself, with the Kickstarter ecosystem providing few backers that you wouldn't have had otherwise. If you could expect to sell $1,000 of your product normally, you might be able to sell $1,000 via Kickstarter. Set your minimum funding goal for $5,000 on the high hopes of reaching new people, and you'll fail, reaching $1,000 but reaping nothing without your minimum met.

We didn't want to sell something in advance. We had an audience, and were (and remain) primarily fiction writers. Writing fiction is *what we want to do.* If we were to be persuaded into diversion, postpone projects we'd been itching to hit, and embark on the technological and administrative hassles of writing a book for an audience, we needed compensation. We didn't want to fund to the tune of a few thousand dollars; we wanted to overfund to the tune of tens of thousands. We got some flack for that, too: people who thought we were being greedy. We didn't agree. In our minds, we were putting on what Sean's then-twelve-year-old daughter, Haley, called "a concert for writing," and no concert performer wants to play a show that merely covers the cost of renting the venue and hiring staff. We wanted to fill every seat in the stadium. If we were going to do this, we wanted the world's attention. We wanted the arena rocking, with thousands of excited, cheering fans.

We'd decided on a minimum funding goal of $19,000, which — considering our costs, delayed income-producing activities, and three partners to split the remains — was the lowest figure we were willing to put on our concert for. But with the video we'd shot — which did a fair job of convincing a buyer to purchase a product but did little to generate a sense of belonging or excitement — we'd be lucky to fund the project, much less shake the chandeliers in a crowded club.

With mere weeks before the deadline to submit our campaign (we had one hole in our schedule for the Kickstarter and another for the project itself), we had to reposition everything.

In the *Fiction Unboxed* story our heroes had experienced their first setback. They'd been seeing the world through their own eyes, but soon faced an epiphany: To help struggling writers, they had to see the world through a struggling writer's eyes. To help experienced writers who'd found themselves tangled in snags, they had to see the world through the eyes of those snagged writers. They couldn't think as Platt and Truant, who'd spent 2013 building worlds with a one and a half million words. They had to slip on another pair of shoes.

So we brainstormed. We stopped asking what instructional material writers wanted and asked ourselves about the problems writers faced. In no time at all, we realized much of what I wrote in this book's carnival barker intro: More than anything, writers face a sense of uncertainty. A sense of being alone. A sense of *having a story inside them that's dying for breath*, but seeing no guideposts to show them how another (nonstruggling) writer might unbox that story, dust it off, and tell it from start to finish.

If we wanted to rock our concert, we had to take that writer by the hand and lead her into the fold. We had to let her watch us in the hopes that she would find the way to her story. From that line of thought, we realized that a world full of writers had been sold on a lie. The "rules" of writing, society, and conditioning have convinced potential raconteurs that storytelling is hard. But it isn't. You simply need to step out of your own way, realize that you already know "story" like the beat of your heart, and that all it takes to change your world with that story is to see how others might handle it. Then you might see that although writing well requires plenty of practice, that practice is like whetting a blade against stone. Our job was to show writers that they carried that blade already, and how we, in our own way, go about drawing it from the sheath.

We shot a new video with a new script, centering on the idea of "changing the world with a story" by freeing writers from their own bullshit. This one was just me and was assembled, scored, and masterfully edited by none other than Kickstarter Guy ZC Bolger's collaborator and our good friend, Garrett Robinson.

With our new video in hand, we started the Kickstarter clock on April 22. We'd learned from some knowledgeable crowdfunding folks that we'd have to drive our own initial traffic to the campaign. If we were lucky, we might go viral on Kickstarter and see new fans arriving. This was a tall order. According to Kickstarter's algorithms, we could only reach that threshold if our project *fully* funded within the first three or four days.

Fully funding that fast was absurd, but we *did* feel confident that we could hit our goal before the funding period ended thirty days later and get to put on our show. We'd get our chance to change the world with a story. We'd be able to do something the world had never seen, and hopefully free a lot of writers' minds in the process.

We were definitely right about that.

Unfortunately, we had no idea what we were getting ourselves into.

APPLY IT! This Chapter's Takeaways and Action Step

Here's the least you need to know from this chapter:

- To tell great stories that resonate you must be willing to face your fears. If a project scares or intimidate you, there's a decent chance that's Destiny's whisper telling you to do it anyway.
- Don't be afraid to do what some people negatively call "flip-flopping." We were skeptical of Kickstarter, but ended up changing our minds. Confident people are unafraid of altering their opinions. Only cowards cling to outdated beliefs just because that's the way things have always been.
- The way you frame a project can mean everything. Always be willing to look at the same thing you've always been doing from a new angle that might better appeal to people who may enjoy or benefit from it.

And here's something you can do RIGHT NOW to apply this chapter's lessons:

- What is the one thing you're most scared to write about? Face your fears by writing a thousand words about exactly that.

CHAPTER THREE:
The Longest Month of Our Lives

FOR OUR REALM & SANDS IMPRINT — where Sean and I make our magic — the end of 2013 had been enchanted by, well, insanity. I'm oddly binary; whereas most people might prefer to stretch their to-dos out into the entire canvas at their disposal, I'll work crazy hard during certain periods if it means I can balance "completely on" with "completely off" times. Even during R&S's period of mad production, I took weekends off and refused to work past 6 p.m., Monday through Friday. I also have certain standing appointments with myself and my family that I refuse to break *during* that work time (I go to the gym three mornings a week and to Barnes & Noble with my kids every Monday), so to make up for it, I'd routinely rise at 4:30 or 5 to write ... then write all day long, working around my self-imposed appointments. For me, this somehow makes sense. On times are on times, and they're *fully* on. Off times, on the other hand, are off times — and are *totally* off.

The end of the year was exhausting, but in the best way. I got to look at my bookshelf and see how we'd closed the core *Unicorn Western* series and written a prequel, how I'd concluded the *Fat Vampire* series, and how we'd found a way to finish full first seasons for our serials *The Beam* and *Robot Proletariat*, our comedies *Greens, Everyone Gets Divorced,* and *Space Shuttle,* and our horror story *Cursed.* Plus two untitled collaborations with Lexi Maxxwell: *The Future of Sex* and *Adult Video*.

But despite all that accomplishment, everything was still kind of in a state of semicompletion. Only one series was fully finished *(Fat Vampire)*, and the others were half-finished. We'd nudged them to sensible, major stopping points at the end of a season, but hadn't closed them entirely. In the middle of the year, we never figured we'd manage to close as many boxes as we did, but had somehow managed it. Somewhat. For a while. Until it was time to ramp up again.

We took two weeks off for the holidays, then jumped up, ready to resume at the start of 2014.

But the first months of 2014, much to our chagrin, ended up being consumed with our first feeble attempts to resurrect our old blogging days — this time with the intention of promoting our fiction. I wrote a ton of what we called epic blog posts, centered on our narrative themes and written to be viral (I'd written several huge hits on my old blog and thought I could transfer that mojo to R&S). Those posts consumed ungodly numbers of hours to get just right.

Sean, on the flip side, was busy developing websites for all our publishing imprints and both podcasts. It made sense at the time — we've always known that our job is to build a great platform and connect with our readers, rather than rely exclusively on retailers like Amazon — but we did it all wrong. The blog posts I'd slaved over were barely shared and didn't come close to justifying the time spent writing them. And all of those websites? They were eventually replaced by our mothership site that included all imprints under one roof: SterlingAndStone.Net.

We were ready for something less riddled with tedium. We were ready to get back to telling all those stories we'd left hanging. We'd done our duty to administrative and marketing chores, but we'd had enough.

Spring of 2014, during which we'd lost so much time, was finally over, and it was time to get back to fiction, where we belonged.

But of course, you already know that's not what happened.

Hangover and Withdrawal

By the time we'd shot our proper Kickstarter video for *Fiction Unboxed* and were starting to tell our audience about the upcoming project and launch date, we had serious nonfiction hangover and accompanying fiction withdrawal. We'd slated a half-dozen fiction projects for early 2014 and were excited about all of them.

But unfortunately, only one (*The Beam's* second season) survived the cuts necessary to make room for all that blogging and web development. Our first-in-series "sci-fi Harry Potter" novel for the Guy Incognito line (*Connor Kwik and the Deadbook Deception*) ended up getting bumped for the second time. We postponed *Unicorn Apocalypse* and the second season of our sleeper hit *Robot Proletariat*. Sean even gave me beats (our form of rough outlines) for the second in our fiction-as-nonfiction series in the world of *The Beam*: a faux treatise on the evolution of human connection called *Sex 2.0* ... but as with everything else, it went into the "eventually" pile to make room for blogging. *The Beam* is a behemoth; it usually requires around three times as long as any other project to get right. And even that one — the single project we finished in the first quarter of the year — was disappointing in its way; the launch date happened to coincide almost exactly with the launch of our Kickstarter, and what should have been the series' triumphant return was more or less lost in the shuffle.

By April of 2014, as the Kickstarter machine was chugging along, more blogging and nonfiction were the last things we wanted. Both of us were starving for story.

But it wasn't quite that simple. We knew we needed to explain our idea for *Fiction Unboxed*, then to explain it another dozen times after that. We'd had such a negative reaction to crowdfunding ourselves that we wanted to do everything in our power to make sure people saw the difference in the way we were using it. The project wasn't charity; it wasn't us asking our audience to "support" us. We weren't pitching a course on how to get rich quick (we loathe the "Kindle gold rush" mentality), and really weren't pitching a *course* at all. As Sean's daughter, Haley, had said, *Fiction Unboxed* was a concert for writing. It was a performance, not instruction. We were going to get on the Internet's stage and do our thing, with our doors and windows (and flies, probably) wide open, and were offering people the chance to watch us live.

I won't go into the abundant details of what we felt we needed to explain here (whether or not people had to watch us live to derive any benefit (no), whether we'd show them how to make money (no), why there were different-priced "backer levels" on Kickstarter for a single project (because like at a concert, seats closer to the stage, where you can see better or mosh with the band, tend to cost more, whereas lawn seats cost very little), but suffice to say there was a lot to communicate. People didn't understand the project's nested nature: Prior to starting our Kickstarter campaign, we had a countdown — meaning we were counting down to a thirty-day funding period that would also then count down to zero ... and only after *that* would we start our book writing project, which of course would itself count down through the thirty days of June.

And perhaps most frustrating of all, we began to get flack from people who thought the whole thing seemed kind of scammy.

They're collecting money to show people how to make a living at writing?

No, we were showing writers how we wrote books.

Their goal is to overfund the Kickstarter campaign?

Fucking-A right, that was our goal. We'd shunted projects aside and were laying our balls on the line, frightened and nervous about being exposed and knowing we might fail publicly. If we were going to do this — if we were going to sell tickets to our concert — was it really a bad thing that we hoped a lot of people would want to watch us? Were they really suggesting we hope *just enough* that people were interested?

More blog posts. More e-mails to our list. More talking about it on *SPP* ... which, in turn, led to more criticism and a rash of bad reviews from people who said, "This podcast used to be great, but now all they do is promote themselves."

By the campaign's first day, we were already sick of it. We were tired of explaining, tired of writing blog posts and other nonfiction, tired of justifying our actions, tired of the entire idea behind *Fiction Unboxed*.

We didn't want to do it anymore. We didn't want to talk about it. We didn't want to detail what the project was versus what it wasn't one more time, and didn't want to hear criticism. We were done. *Done.*

But fortunately, within minutes of Sean pushing Kickstarter's go button at 9 a.m. Eastern Standard Time on

Tuesday, April 22, a group of amazing people immediately changed our minds.

Amazeballs

I didn't keep a record of what happened that morning, but the first thing I remember seeing was a Tweet from podcast listener Mgon ("EM-gee-on"; we had to ask him), who wrote something like:

FICTION UNBOXED IS LIVE WOOOOOOOOOO!!!

I might not have the correct number of o's, and Mgon may have added a few of his trademark "heart" characters to the Tweet (check out the supporters list at the back of the completed *Dream Engine* novel; his heart is the first thing you'll see on the page), but it's in the ballpark.

I looked at the campaign page, pausing that day's writing to do so, and never went back.

Within three minutes, half a dozen people had backed *Fiction Unboxed*. That was impressive. Far MORE impressive, *we hadn't even told anyone that the campaign was live*. It was just after 8:30 EST, and our "go live" loudly announced on *SPP* wasn't until 10 a.m. We'd wanted that first hour to iron out any problems that might occur, to show it to a few eager personal friends, and so on. Our e-mail was queued but unsent, with a half-dozen backers already on board.

I texted Sean:

Holy shit. They've just been refreshing Kickstarter, waiting.

Sean texted back:

We're already up to $500!

And Mgon Tweeted:

$750 GO BABY GO WOO-HOO!!

The next hour turned to a memory in minutes as I stared. Kickstarter makes this easy, updating without your having to reload the page.

The first inklings of crowdfunding's inherent flaw prickled within me, as Mgon and a dozen other *SPP* die-hards updated our totals live on Twitter like play-by-play announcers rattling stats around dollar signs. But during those first few hours, I didn't care. I was excited about *Fiction Unboxed* again — not because we were making money, but *because our fans were behind us.* We'd taken some punches in the lead-up, and because critics tend to be loud it's easy to feel like they're the majority. But on that April morning, the *Self-Publishing Podcast* community showed us that a massive majority was excited about the project ... and that *they* could shake the rafters, too.

By 10 a.m. Eastern, we were already 20 percent funded. We sent an e-mail to the *Unboxed* early notification list and began chattering on social media. Totals climbed faster. We'd created 300 "early bird" slots in our campaign that amounted to a $10 discount, and they immediately started to vanish. I remember hoping that we hadn't underestimated demand sufficient to piss off people on the West Coast, who might wake at a reasonable hour to find that our early birds had eaten all the worms.

We watched it grow.

And when I say we, I don't mean me, Sean, and Dave. I mean *all of us*. I mean *the entire SPP community*. I've never before seen anyone rally for something I helped to create in quite the same way. *Fans were acting as if Fiction Unboxed belonged to them.* I cringed at fans reporting dollars on Twitter (that's taunting the haters!), while marveling that it was being done with nothing but pride. The campaign belonged to *us*.

Twitter cheered.

Facebook cheered.

Kickstarter has its own comments ecosystem, and new comments appeared at each milestone: Almost $5000! Almost 50 percent! Who will tip it to five figures? One more person to get us to 700 backers!

They said *WE*. They said *US*. And these people were already in; they weren't going to benefit any more if the project overfunded (well, they did, but nobody knew that yet). They were *happy for us*. They were cheering us like a favorite sports team at the championship game.

I was suddenly dying to open my office doors and windows for these people. None of us could wait to move past the funding campaign and start the project. Sean was his usual Labrador self in our texts, and even Dave was using exclamation points. He typically saves that particular punctuation for complaining about people shopping all wrong while at Target.

The campaign had fully funded before the eleventh hour elapsed. Our project turned from prospective and conditional to a certainty. I remember being happy, but feeling all celebrated out already. It had been an emotionally exhausting day, because the rallying and cheering had never stopped. Our Kickstarter stream was hundreds of comments long, and our Twitter feeds were jammed. Fans of Team *SPP* had been clapping and shouting and doing a stadium wave through the entire day. We'd been beside them, doing the same.

We were happy. Flattered. Humbled. We didn't have the energy to be nervous; we were too blissed in a soporific afterglow.

It was over. We'd done it.

And yet, it wasn't over at all.

We had many promises to keep, and miles to run before sleeping.

A Marathon, Not a Sprint

Imagine getting excited. You're thrilled. You're jazzed. You've been waiting for whatever it is, and that thing is finally here. Clap your hands. Stomp your feet. Shout your heart out; raise the roof. Cheer and holler. Pump your fists in the air! Jump up and down; chest-bump your neighbor; thrash around and scream and shout.

Now, keep it up for a month.

That's the way our campaign felt after the first twenty-four hours. We woke to new Tweets and fresh Facebook messages, a few enthusiastic Kickstarter comments. Mgon kept sending campaign updates as if we were on a mountaintop unable to check for ourselves. On that second morning, we squinted at those revelers, with bleary eyes and mugs of coffee clenched in sleepy hands, and mumbled, "You guys are still awake?"

The first day's success had been meteoric. We'd thought it seemed crazy to fund in three or four days. We'd done it in eleven hours. The *Fiction Unboxed* campaign had leapt onto Kickstarter's front page, topping every nested category. We had earned the exposure we'd wanted, and more. We woke to find ourselves significantly over 100 percent funding, but the frenzy was a little more muted, like how each touchdown following an obvious landslide gathers a few less cheers.

I wrote that day. Not a lot, but some. The next day I wrote a little more, and was back to full speed — business as unusual — within the week. Frenzy fell to the background, and we checked our progress less frequently, being sure to throw our hands in the air and hoot with the crowd when another milestone was hit.

But day to day, maintaining that level of enthusiasm was exhausting. Sean and I had both been part of Internet launches before, but they typically last only a few days and even then leave you drained. During a launch, you need to keep stoking promotional fires. You have to keep banging the drum and adding sugar to the pot. And if you can manage, you must do it all without feeling like (or looking like) a total whore.

The concept of "stretch goals" are one of the things about Kickstarter that we'd anticipated but failed to fully grasp. Stretch goals are milestones you set above and beyond your initial funding target. Hitting them encourages new backers to join, current backers to up their backing level, and interested folks to help spread your word. You're basically saying, "You've green-lit the project. Now, while we're at it, would you like to green-light this 'project enhancement' too?"

Every day, we looked for ways to tweak and improve the campaign. We couldn't rest while the clock was still ticking. Which stretch goal could we add, and how could we communicate it to backers and prospective backers without (hopefully) annoying them? Whom else could we tell about the project, and how could we get press? Were our stretch goals exciting?

We made a mistake about that last one early on, promising "transcripts of the podcast, episodes one through twenty-five" if the project hit $25,000. We hit the goal, and backers responded with a grateful *Meh*. We had to shuffle our goals, suddenly aware that no one gave the smallest of shits about transcripts, and communicate the change. Our next goal, at $35,000, was far more interesting to backers: a free copy of our favorite writing software, Scrivener, which is something we all swear by (and can't live without). At $50,000 we promised to write our new novel as "open-source fiction" (complete with a comprehensive "world history and conventions" Scrivener template), which allowed anyone to write in our story world and keep 100 percent of the money for themselves. At $60,000, we promised a popular training series called Learn Scrivener Fast.

Every few days, we posted Kickstarter updates, promising more. We had stretch goals to deliver and promises to keep. And we had gifts to give: items added to backer reward levels "just because," without requiring a goal to meet. There's an etiquette to Kickstarter, and it's more complicated than keeping your napkin on your lap and being sure to use the proper fork at the proper time.

Communicate, communicate, communicate.

Promote, promote, promote.

Give, give, give.

And in addition to all that, we were supposed to be spreading word to our networks — and, ideally, the wider press. We thought the story was newsworthy: Who else had ever written a full novel, from start to finish, while raw and exposed? We were breaking paradigms. We were demystifying the mysterious. We were, probably, likely to be seen by some as giving away the magicians' secrets. We expected pushback. We expected other writers to hate on us, to say we were hacks and didn't know what we were talking about.

We didn't expect such a deafening silence.

The campaign taught us some unforgettable lessons. And although *Fiction Unboxed*'s Kickstarter was wildly successful, we made a few mistakes that either carried a negative impact (keeping the campaign from reaching its full potential) or stayed in neutral (costing us too much time and effort for zero return):

MISTAKE #1: We Talked About the Platform, Not the Story

Sean and I, who share a robust network of influential friends and a knack for attracting attention, created a long list of people who might help us spread word about *Fiction Unboxed* and create a viral, newsworthy buzz that would send it over the top. It was, in fact, mostly the same system we used to launch *Write. Publish. Repeat.*, a book that exceeded all our expectations.

Here's how all of the e-mails and pitches to those people began:

"We're doing a Kickstarter campaign for a project in which we'll write a book live, from scratch, in thirty days, in front of an audience, with nothing held back!"

Did you spot our mistake?

We didn't see it at first, but in retrospect it's obvious and *still* makes us feel like total assholes. We ourselves got what I described as "douche chills" when we first thought about Kickstarter, but forgot all about our first impressions in the thrill of our exciting plans. Now it's clear that our contacts heard this:

"We're doing a Kickstarter campaign *womp womp womp douche womp womp.*"

You know that noise adults make in the Peanuts cartoons? That's what people heard in their heads once we said Kickstarter campaign. They stopped listening, because it sounded like we were begging for money.

We should have said: "We're doing a project in which we'll write a book live, from scratch, in thirty days, in front of an audience, with nothing held back!"

If they asked how we were funding it, we could say, "Oh, we're doing it via Kickstarter because it allows us to gauge interest in advance, blah blah blah who cares about that part."

The uneasy feeling I got the moment our fans were loudly cheering our progress on social media was this inkling exactly, and it's an unfortunate crowdfunding truism: *In any crowdfunding campaign, the only measuring stick that anyone looks at, discusses, cares about, or really pays any attention to is how much money you're making.*

Our fans "got it" enough to see past that; most people didn't.

By leading with the platform rather than with the amazing *Fiction Unboxed* story (first of its kind, demystifying storytelling, freeing writers' minds, and so on), we barred paths of promotion that may have stayed open otherwise — people who looked at our e-mails and said, "Oh, they just want me to help them raise money."

SEAN PLATT & JOHNNY B. TRUANT

MISTAKE #2: We Spent Our Social Capital Foolishly

The P.S. on the above point is that once we realized what some people must have thought of our e-mails, we felt like total dickheads because we realized at least some of them must have seen us that way.

We contacted our friend David Gaughran, who runs the popular *Let's Get Digital* self-publishing blog, to talk about *Unboxed* early on. We figured it was a mutually beneficial proposition; David likes us, likes our work (his review of *Write. Publish. Repeat.* is currently the book's "most helpful" on Amazon, and he praised *WPR* extensively on his blog), and his audience should be intrigued by the *Unboxed* story. But when he got back to us, sort of hemming and hawing, acting like someone who wanted to help on principle but was reluctant to do so in practice, at least we could see the problem. David shot straight with us and helped us see how this all must appear. With others, we weren't as lucky. We fear that with those people we may have come off like needy, greedy assholes ... but never had a chance to fully explain ourselves and rectify that impression.

By the time we realized our error, we still had time to pre-guess David's true objection and stop him from helping us out "just to be nice." We sent him a "we're letting you off the hook; no worries" e-mail. I could practically hear his sigh of relief all the way from Prague.

You only have so much social capital, and it spends like money. Use up your social capital asking for dumb things in stupid ways, and you'll end up broke with nothing tangible. Most of our e-mails about *Unboxed* — even some sent to friends — went unanswered.

People didn't even bother to respond.

The tragedy isn't that we felt slighted; it's that we began to feel that the lack of response was because people thought we were (say it with me) needy, greedy assholes. We didn't get any promotion and felt like we burned bridges for nothing. In reality, we probably merely *singed* those bridges, but still we saw some of our hard earned social capital swirling down the drain.

Social capital is the lifeblood of your reputation. Always spend wisely, in anticipation of mutual benefit. Never waste it foolishly or without considering what you might gain from the expense.

MISTAKE #3: We Spent Far Too Much Time and Effort Outside Our Tribe

All that social capital we spent? It cost us a ton of time, tremendous effort, and an ugly in our guts. Sean hates asking people for things. *Hates it.* It's a side effect of his generosity, which teeters on too giving. I'm less reticent, but those "asks" still cost us a lot, and left us with icky feelings in the end.

What kills us, though, is that *those asks weren't even remotely necessary.* We spent all that time, effort, and icky feelings for nothing, because the vast, vast, *vast* majority of enthusiasm for and activity around *Fiction Unboxed* came from our own tribe — from, in other words, the people whose attention we already had, and whom we didn't need to expend any extra effort to reach.

We did meet a few amazing people through Kickstarter and our outside-the-*SPP*-tribe marketing (hi, Kayla and Kalvin!), but we estimate that we could have achieved 90 percent of *Fiction Unboxed*'s final result by doing nothing more than sending a few e-mails to our existing list and discussing the project on our podcast — then selling it directly from our website, eschewing Kickstarter and all those stretch goals and updates. I'm not being hyperbolic: *90 percent of the result likely came from 10 percent of the effort.* Thinking about the waste — especially given the novels we sidelined to make the project happen — is humbling.

Oh, and another thing? We also spent cold, hard cash on a few promotions for *Unboxed* in addition to organic outreach. We were so convinced that the story had "OMG!" potential that we were willing to pony up for a high-end targeted press release, Facebook ads, and a social media blitz through a service called Thunderclap, running us nearly $1,500.

Total return, being generous, based on activity at the time: *Maaaaaaybe* $100. *Maybe.*

Nothing flopped harder than those ads. It was almost a straight line on a graph: the further we went from the audience we already had, the less success we saw.

Trimming the Tribe

We made a lot of mistakes throughout our campaign — but paradoxically, some things that might look like mistakes from the outside were intentional.

We did fail to position the campaign right when we promoted outside our tribe, but we feel great about the way we communicated within the *SPP* community. We told our core group, adequately and often, about what *Fiction Unboxed* was and why they should care. We answered questions, addressed objections, and spoke openly about the process of building the campaign, what we hoped to get from the project as creators and businessmen, and what we intended to give. We were open books — just like protagonists, within the *Unboxed* story, who spoke their minds without hesitation or fear.

We discussed the campaign as it rolled along — maybe too much, in the minds of some.

We were excited about it as a business venture and expressed our hopes for high funding — which, to some, surely made us look greedy.

Of the three of us, Dave is by far the most concerned about alienating people and giving them "the wrong impression." I put that in quotes because to Sean and me, it's not the wrong impression at all. We *were* excited about our project. We *did* want to talk about it. We *did* hope it would be a home run, and yes, we (for shame!) *did* hope it would make us plenty of money.

The *Unboxed* promotion period made Dave nervous because he was sure we were alienating people and losing podcast listeners. He was convinced that people would resent us, think we were charlatans ... perhaps even *hate* us.

It was hard for us to assuage Dave's fears, because we agreed with him 100 percent.

Whenever you begin any venture — be it selling a product or writing a novel — you have two choices: you can try to appeal to everyone and offend no one, or you can stay true to your internal compass, say what you truly mean, and accept that some people won't like it.

We have always chosen the latter, because timidity is not a good trait for any creative person. Bland, hesitant art is the most banal and uninteresting thing in the world. Bland paintings are purchased for $5 and hang above couches in waiting rooms. Bland music is played in elevators. Bland books earn indifference. Only art that polarizes people — that forces an audience to choose one side or the other, daring anyone to stay in the antiseptic center — can also move them. Only art with the capacity to stir dislike and hate truly contains the potential to be loved. It's only *that* kind of art — that which you like or dislike, love or hate, adore with all your heart or hate with vitriol — that's worth creating.

So yes, some people hated *Fiction Unboxed* from the start, just like a few people truly hated *Write. Publish. Repeat.* But we didn't want to be safe; we wanted to make art worth making.

We said to Dave, "Let some people hate us. Let some people feel we're greedy, or charlatans, or scammers. We're going to lose some people no matter what we do, just as we'd lose people by never doing anything interesting. So let's at least choose whom we alienate. Let's pick our side, and decide which fans we want to speak to. Then let's speak to them and ignore the boos from the cheap seats in the back."

Why? Because we knew the roar from those True Fans in the front could swallow the boos, if we stayed authentic to ourselves — and to them. We'd seen as much in those first eleven hours of the campaign, and were continuing to see it each and every day.

"More.

Higher.

We can do it!"

That wasn't us shouting for *Fiction Unboxed*'s success. Those were our fans. Those were the people we'd earned *specifically* by turning away from a small minority of haters.

Through the campaign's long and final push, those true fans buoyed us and kept our spirits high. We definitely had down times, when e-mails told us to stop yammering on and a rash of one-star reviews appeared on our podcast's iTunes page. We had long, painful days when criticism reared its ugly head, and we were asked to defend ourselves like a naughty child being called to the principal's office. But in the end, once those negative waves rolled onto a forgotten shore, it didn't matter. You can't live your life to avoid barbs from a few sour apples. Doing so is an insult to your art, to yourself, and to the majority who love what you do. If you want to have True Fans, you will always pay with an occasional hater. Remember that.

The Kickstarter's third-to-last day crawled into the second-to-last day, leaving a snail trail behind it, with all three of us riding the final dip of an emotional roller coaster. The last day came slowest, and in the final hours the clock seemed to freeze. We were exhausted. *Happy. Thrilled. Over the moon.* But beat.

The *SPP* community cheered harder, urging a final push.

The Kickstarter clock, just to make things more unbearable, counted the final minutes down by the second.

Three, two, one.

A cheer arose. I'm not making this up. *People went on social media and cheered.*

Zero.

Time ran out, and *Fiction Unboxed* became the third-most-successful fiction campaign on Earth in Kickstarter's history — closing at 355% funded for a grand total of $67,535.

We had just shy of a thousand backers — all fans, purified of haters — eager to see us tell our story.

The comments stopped tallying the project's total, and the ticking clock instead turned to a new question. That question was practically audible in its enthusiasm, each commenter chewing the bit with excitement:

"When can we start?"

APPLY IT! This Chapter's Takeaways and Action Step

Here's the least you need to know from this chapter:

- It's easy to sell something that people actually want. Put your reader's needs before your own and keep asking what would serve them best.

- Know what you're doing and *why*. A Kickstarter campaign isn't for everyone, nor is every story. Know what you expect to get out of a project before you start, never acting simply because "everyone says it's a good idea." We had specific aims for our project, and knew what we were willing to do to reach our desired outcomes.

- Understand that "story" is part of everything you do. Kickstarter became part of our story, and our story informed the Kickstarter campaign. (You'll see this theme recur during the actual Fiction Unboxed writing project, when we incorporated true-life events from this phase of our stories into our actual fiction.)

- Don't underestimate your tribe. It's always best to nurture your existing readers than it is to go out and find new ones. Yes, you always want to expand your reach, but it's more important to love the ones you're with and let them help you to grow, and to spend most of your time focused on them, not new people.

- Be clear in the story you want to tell ("we're writing a book in 30 days" rather than "we're running a Kickstarter") and those inclined to love it will be more likely to respond.
- Never be afraid to trim your tribe.
- Always over-deliver on your promises. We constantly added bonuses and goals throughout the campaign, and charged much less for the base access level of *Unboxed* than it was worth. It may have cost us revenue on a per-person basis, but our tribe appreciated it, spread word about our project, and supported us more than we ever imagined.

And here's something you can do RIGHT NOW to apply this chapter's lessons:

- Design a fake crowd funding campaign for a book you really want to write. In designing this fake campaign, don't be afraid to "trim the tribe" and cull the people who are unlikely to enjoy your story from the project. (**NOTE:** We don't especially like the idea of crowdfunding individual novels, so we're not suggesting you actually run this campaign, though that's of course your decision to make. The idea is to design the campaign as an exercise to help clarify your story.)

PART TWO:
FICTION UNBOXED

CHAPTER FOUR:
Building Our World

USUALLY, KICKSTARTER CAMPAIGNS RAISE FUNDS for something far in advance of its creation. The model is, "You fund it, then they make it." Fund a gadget, and the creator goes out and gets the gadget fabricated. Fund a movie, and the movie must be made. If you fund a book, the book must be written. But in most cases, you, as a Kickstarter backer, need to be patient as you wait for your rewards. It's often months or even years before you get what you're owed.

That wasn't the case for *Fiction Unboxed*. The funding period ended on May 22, and we knew that on June 1 we had to show up for work. But even then, it wasn't about hitting the lab to make what people were due. Because they were going to be *watching* us in that lab, we had to build it first. We had to get all the right locks on its doors, and hand out keys. We had to paint the lab and make it presentable. And we had to make it comfortable, because people were going to be there a while.

Even though we said from the start that people didn't need to watch *Fiction Unboxed* in real time (people who "Unbox" from our site now certainly don't), there was a huge upswell during that first wave of folks who wanted to anyway. In addition to simply preparing to plan, write, edit, polish, and publish a full-length novel in a month (a process that normally takes us three times as long, with multiple in-progress works overlapping), we had to build a membership website where Unboxers could watch our meetings, read our words, and generally peek over our shoulders. They asked for forums to discuss the event as it happened, and to meet each other, so we gave them forums. We had to effectively communicate with our newest community and deliver owed items, so we had to wrangle that. And on and on and on.

If April 22 to May 22 was a marathon, May 22 to May 31 was a sprint. We churned and churned, trying to get everything ready in time for our thirty-day experiment. Most of the grunt work fell to Sean, while Dave and I were there to test sequence and flow, making sure everything worked right and that nothing was going to break. I, meanwhile, was trying to clear my plate. I was writing *Connor Kwik* at the time, and poor Connor had already suffered flow issues as my focus flickered through May. With the June 1 deadline looming, I was rushing to finish it so that *Blunderbuss* — which was the ridiculous name Sean used for "untitled novel to be conceived and written during *Fiction Unboxed* because I have to call it *something*" — would have my full attention. I didn't make it. When June started, with all of us running around with our hair on fire, I had to set Connor aside with less than a week's worth of work remaining. It's still unfinished.

On May 31, we recorded a "Day Zero" video to explain what viewers (or listeners or readers — however they chose to consume the content) should expect. We told people, "We really have no idea how this is all going to work, so let's find out together."

The next day, on Day One, we began to build our book's world.

And as we did, we found out just how true that statement was.

Day One

Normally, ideas simmer in our heads for weeks, months ... sometimes years before we draw them out to craft a story from that raw hunk of clay. There's one upcoming trilogy — *Unicorn Apocalypse*, which will close the box on the *Unicorn Western* universe — that Sean has been using as a mental dumping ground for over a year as I write this. I have no idea if he actually keeps a file of notes on the ideas he wants to use, but I can't talk to Sean for too long before he'll start telling me about how some appliance shop in Austin will be an old hitching post in *Apocalypse*, or how a plot involving Hatch chilis (a Southwest staple that Sean may have had baked into his bread that morning) will foil our gunslinger Clint and his trusty (but testy) steed, Edward, as they try to save the worlds from collapse.

But on Day One of *Fiction Unboxed*, we had none of those seeds between us. In fact, there was one seed that Sean had been nursing because he has to nurse *something* at all times — the vaguest sort of vague idea for a world our story *might* inhabit — that he'd refused to tell me about even though he blabbered to one of our listeners, Ephraim, at a conference in May. When the Day One meeting began, we were colder than freezing. We were icebergs with nothing to start a fire. It immediately hit us, just how crazy our undertaking was.

We had zero idea about the story we might tell.

We had zero idea of the world that story might inhabit.

We had a thousand people watching every move we made.

And not only were we under the gun to produce a finished novel before the end of the month, we'd also promised a fleshed-out story world large enough for all our Unboxers to write their own stories in, if they chose to do so.

If you're not familiar with the idea of a "story world," here's how that works — whether you do open-source fiction like we did (where others can write in your world, keeping all the sales proceeds for themselves) or simply write in it yourself:

Every story takes place in a world. Many stories take place in the everyday world we see around us — a world where there are seven continents, men, women, and children, and unrest in the Middle East. Most literary fiction takes place in that world. A story might be set in Paris or Bangladesh, but neither of those places are the world. They're just a corner of the world, and though you may not ever hear about Paris in a Bangladesh story or vice-versa, *there is a Paris* in the Bangladesh story. It exists, in other words, because it's part of the world, whether the reader sees it or not.

On the far opposite end of the spectrum, fantasy and sci-fi novels tend to take place in unreal worlds that are, to a greater or lesser degree, conjured by the authors. There are many ways to shuffle this deck of cards, and you may end up in our actual world as we imagine it in the future (like in our serial *The Beam*), a world that is more or less normal and present day but inhabited by mystical creatures (most urban fantasy), or a world that is "our world as far as you know." Our serial *Robot Proletariat* is this way, albeit in the future. You might ask if *Robot Proletariat* is set in Britain, and we'd tell you, "We don't know. Sure. For now." Because until we have need to explain more of the world than the single residence that harbors Season 1, we've left that to the aether.

There's a mishmash in between. But every world — including the real one — has rules. Dave likes to define his world in advance, drawing maps if necessary so he knows where his characters are and what they'll encounter if headed west. I prefer to start bare bones and discover the world as I go, as we did with the rather complicated fantasy world (complete with religions, rituals, and all sorts of metaphysical rules) of *Unicorn Western*. Sean straddles the middle. For many stories, he's let me explore. But before I began work on *The Beam*, I was given a document as detailed as a set of zoning laws. I knew a *lot* about that world before the first page, complete with its history from the present until the story's starting year of 2097.

Because of the stepwise nature of *Fiction Unboxed* — and our promise to build a world for Unboxers as we crafted our tale — we'd decided to devote the first day to brainstorming about the world itself. To me, this felt backward, but what the hell? The whole thing was strange.

On Day Zero, once we settled in and kinda-sorta-not-really forgot about the cameras and tried to pretend we were alone, Sean gave Dave and me the tagline he'd given Ephraim in May:

"It's 'steampunk *Lord of the Rings*.'"

Dave, who was going to join us for the world brainstorming before fading into the background to mock or ignore us, immediately objected to this, as he does most things.

In the same voice he'd used to say, "Do you know even what color smoke came out of guns back then?" to dismiss Sean's desire to write a western and give us the idea for *Unicorn Western* in one fell swoop, Dave said, "Have either of you ever even *read* a steampunk book?"

We had, but it didn't matter. Steampunk — a genre that wonders what the world would be like if it had continued to embrace steam and clockwork power instead of being distracted by the microchip — was, to Sean and me, an aesthetic. We weren't worried about "conforming to the rules of steampunk." What creative person gets all wrapped up in rules? We flapped our hands at Dave's silliness and said that we'd watched movies, we'd seen photos, we'd read a few books.

Big, steam-powered machines.

Clockwork anachronisms.

Corsets, goggles, and leather.

Got it.

But that was where Sean's prep stopped: at that single tagline. Imagine *Lord of the Rings*, complete with elves and wizards and trolls and other fantasy tropes. Now marry it to steampunk. *Boom.*

The reason Sean liked the world, though, was because it could be huge. If people wanted an open world to play in, this world cracked like a walnut. Did you want to write a romance? Fine, tell an elfin love story. Did you want to tell a sci-fi story? Fine, use wizards or clockwork time machines — or, for that matter, steam-powered starships. Want to write a horror story? Then head down the mines where the trolls live and knock yourself out.

The playground was open for business.

For days, we'd had Unboxers knocking on our inbox doors, rattling the forums, and tapping us on the shoulder whenever we showed our faces on Twitter. They were jonesing; they were ready. They were anticipating a story that we still hadn't started, and we could feel their excited eyes on us as we rolled Sean's idea around in our heads. Would people be excited about that world? Yes, we thought they would be.

What followed on Day One was a delightful mishmash. Sean's first pitch was that in this steampunky world that somehow had unicorns and stuff in it (but maybe not mermaids; for some reason Dave had a problem with mermaids), our story could take place in an isolated kingdom. A very long time ago, real history forked away from our imagined history as flight was discovered early, by a Da Vinci-type character. Flight provided might, and the kingdom got all uppity and tyrannical as it enforced its air superiority on the rest of the world.

Dave piped up. He proposed that maybe a rebel group or nation could decide to one-up the flight-superior kingdom ... by "going old-school" and training dragons.

Looking back now that *The Dream Engine* (the rather "steampunk *Lord of the Rings*" book we ended up writing) is finished, it's fascinating to see how many sparks of later ideas appeared on that first day. For instance:

• There were no dragon riders in our story (yet), and there was nothing special about the history of flight, but dragons *do* play a large role in our finished book. For one, our protagonist, Eila, is afraid of fire, and the nightmarescape of "the Fog" is plagued by dragons for her — not to mention the fact that Eila's manifesting a dragon in the world is the event that causes our kingdom's walls to start crumbling.

• While discussing the different stories that could be told in the world, I for some reason immediately jumped on the notion of a "steampunk asylum," which showed up later as Joffrey Columns.

• From the get-go, Sean proposed that a cool last-page reveal in our book would be to have a character walk up on an unbelievable sight that made their breath catch in their throat — the kind of world-changing sight that showed them how much larger the world was than their own tiny kingdom, though they'd never known it before. And while we didn't do it on *The Dream Engine's* final page, it was very near the end and a large part of the book's original, faulty ending. (More about that faulty ending and the trouble it caused later.)

• And lastly, Sean already had an idea for a name for the "kingdom" we were considering — a name that later became the name of Eila's country. He liked "Alterra," after the brand of coffee served in his apartment building's clubhouse.

We ended Day One feeling great but disorganized, which was about what we'd expected. A full two hours had yielded no coherent plot ideas, no real genre for our specific story, not a single character, and only the vaguest idea of the world we'd end up with. But that was okay. The ball was rolling, and our job on Day Two was to firm up that world enough for Sean to start sketching the story's outline.

Day Two

I can only imagine what our Unboxers, watching the process of live, unscripted brainstorming, must have thought as they saw us stumble through those first couple of days.

Day One was a mess, not at all surprising given that Dave and I were starting from zero and Sean was starting from a five-word phrase worthy of inclusion on a movie poster. But while it's cute and neat to pull a tagline from a movie's feel and plot to slap on a poster, everyone assumes that the movie is done by the time you do that. Ours wasn't.

To use one of Sean's favorite words, we only had "vapor." We were trying to reverse engineer the movie from the tagline, and we were all over the place as a result.

Remember, at this point in the process, the book didn't even have a name. How could it? There wasn't even a plot. For months, we'd been calling it *Blunderbuss* as a sort of dummy title because although it was vapor, it was still listed on the Realm & Sands production calendar. We still had to discuss it among ourselves ("We can't start *Robot Proletariat Season Two* during that time period ... we'll be writing *Blunderbuss!*" and "Do we want to buy ads to promote the *Blunderbuss* launch?"), and we still wanted to talk about it on the podcast. Sean often forgets that not everyone knows the contents of his mind in the latter case, so there were many moments during April, May, and June when I felt compelled to step in and explain what the hell he meant when he kept riffing about this *Blunderbuss* thing. ("He means the novel we'll write during *Fiction Unboxed,* which doesn't have a name yet," I'd elaborate. Which, incidentally, wasn't any less confusing for listeners.)

So there we were on Day Two, organizing the mess of Day One in the sense that a person organizes a movie he's watching by resuming it after a break to make popcorn. Because even though "organizing our thoughts" was the plan for Day Two, all we really did was to *continue* Day One's raw pile-making. And what's more — spoiler alert — the transition from Day Two into Day Three was mostly the same.

Like I said, I can only imagine what the audience must have thought. We'd planned to devote Day One to "world stuff" and Day Two to "genre and plot ideas." But Day Two resumed with more disorder, none of it gelling into anything remotely coherent.

All three of us liked the idea of "steampunk *Lord of the Rings*," but to us it broke down like this:

1. *LORD OF THE RINGS* = There are fantasy creatures in the world, but
2. STEAMPUNK = We can explain those creatures through science.

I suppose that's why we veered so heavily into the idea of "genetic manipulation" by underground "dirty scientists" in Day One: We needed a way to explain all those trolls, dwarves, elves, unicorns, and (sorry, Dave) mermaids. But as had been the case all through Day One, we just kind of swirled around the idea, then whooshed away into something else without deciding anything.

You know why they call it brainstorming, right? Because it has all the sense and order of a storm. Never in my writing life has this been truer.

We hit a lot of other notions during Day Two, none of which resolved any more than the genetic manipulation thing. (Which, by the way, I derailed myself. I have a degree in genetics, and I wasn't buying the idea of a steam-and-clockwork gene sequencer. If this world didn't have the electronics required for automated genetics work, their machines would require some magic.)

So we discussed magic, in the form of an enchanted element or holy stones. We careened into the idea of a purge in the past that left one special person with magic in their bloodline — a purge committed by the government to rid itself of threats, and a person now able to topple that government. *But what if there were two people with such a trait,* we wondered. *A boy and a girl. They could each be carriers of*

SEAN PLATT & JOHNNY B. TRUANT

whatever this trait is, and the dirty scientists could be trying to pair them, knowing their offspring would have powers.

That led Sean into the idea of doing "steampunk *Romeo and Juliet*," which Unboxers roundly hated in the forums afterward but I secretly thought could be awesome — if we didn't simply recapitulate Baz Luhrmann's 1996 film *Romeo + Juliet* and instead used that old story's framework rather than its literal content.

Then somehow, halfway through the session, something magic happened, though it's only magic in retrospect.

During brainstorming, most of our sentences start with "what if." And at some point, out of the blue, this happened:

> SEAN: "This is a totally different direction, but what if science in this world has managed a way to actualize dreams? So if someone can dream something, they can manifest that into reality."
>
> DAVE: "I was thinking of the song, 'Dream with Me.'"
>
> SEAN: "So they have people who are like power-er dreamers, who ... It's almost like 3-D printing or some shit. They put the power dreamers in there. They manipulate their dreams, they train them to dream a certain way. I don't know exactly where I'm going with this, but I like the idea ..."

(I've been sure to include Dave's aside because it's so characteristic. At various points in our podcast Dave has sung "Free Bird," "People are People," "Every Breath You Take," and many more.)

Now, in case you don't know the framing of *The Dream Engine* (which was the title that finally, blessedly, replaced *Blunderbuss* in the second half of *Unboxed*), it's about a society that manifests what it needs directly from the minds of a psychically gifted class of workers. So this was it. This was the spark where everything started.

We must have known it, too, because we swarmed around the idea of dream actualization — which, naturally, would be aided by a massive steam-and-clockwork engine. We knew we wanted the fantasy elements too, so we started to play with the idea that "lights of fancy and even nightmare creatures might be manifested by accident or as inevitable waste during this society's usual process, much like nuclear fission produces nuclear waste. They'd be discarded. Perhaps they'd return seeking revenge.

We wondered if there would be Dream Police (and Dave launched into singing a few bars of the Cheap Trick song).

We wondered if there would be "designated dreamers," and if their job would be akin to a mental violation, or torture. Dave seized on the "precogs" from *Minority Report* as a loose comparison.

We figured that in such a society, a lot of anthropology, technology, and social conventions would stem from the fact that dreams were constantly mined and stolen. How many people would try to resist dream theft? Would a constantly raked population develop a dreaming callus that necessitated the use of more extreme dream-invasion measures to meet society's requirements? And perhaps the most interesting question: If this world was able to harvest creativity directly from the subconscious minds of its citizens, would people's ability to solve problems and think critically while they were awake start to atrophy? Because if they can tap directly into creativity's unfiltered source by plumbing the mind, why would anyone bother to invent anything the hard way?

We ended Day Two energized, excited to see what Day Three might bring. We had a ton of great ideas on the table, but unfortunately none were anywhere near what Sean needed to start shaping a narrative. We decided that instead of paring our brainstorming group down from three to two — moving from a trio to just Sean and me, who would do the actual book-writing — we'd invite Dave back for Day Three.

Sean would work up some very rough concepts: the loosest of loose kinds of story ideas.

He wanted to work up a world timeline, incorporating what we'd discussed. From there, we could begin to get a feel for the characters we might want to follow, the tale we wanted to tell. It would mean delaying plot discussions for another day, but the result would be worth it.

Dave and I couldn't wait to see what Sean would pull out of all of Day Two's awesomeness and bring to us. The skies were sunny with excitement ahead.

We never saw the ugly and demoralizing session coming.

Day Three

On the morning of Day Three, I got this text from Sean:

> This is so amazing. If you don't love what I've come up with, I'm going to cry. Not really but LOL.

And, recalling the ridiculous premises Sean had given me thus far ("It's like *The Fugitive*, but with a chupacabra!" or "It's *Downton Abbey* with robots!"), I texted back:

> I think at this point we've established that there's nothing you can pitch me that I'm not going to think is awesome.

And that's the spirit with which I entered Day Three's meeting, joining Dave to see what Sean had come up with for our story's timeline: thrilled, giddy, and eager.

If only things had stayed that way.

The first thing Sean gave us, after preliminaries were out of the way, was a question: "Have you ever heard of the Akashic records?"

Dave and I had no idea, but trusted that Sean would show us how whatever it was tied into our story seeds from the day before.

"They're a record of the collective unconscious — everything that anyone in the world has ever thought or will think, or has happened or could happen."

The noises Dave and I made at this point were the politer equivalents of "*Oooooo-kaaaay ...* " We had no idea where Sean was going, but he'd been at the last meeting same as we had. He was a smart guy who paid attention. Surely this was going to tie into dream extraction, genetic manipulation, a society where pseudo-precogs were tortured into manifesting what society needed, maybe a Romeo and Juliet vibe. *Right?*

But instead of hitting any of that, Sean went on to explain that thousands and thousands of years ago, there were terrestrials (giant creatures made of earth) and celestials (which were basically elves, from the heavens). At the yearly solstices, these two races met, combined in a ceremony Sean termed nativity, then mutually annihilated into a substance called Crumble.

The *Fiction Unboxed* transcripts don't include psychic transmissions for some reason, but luckily I have a record of them. Here's a snippet.

> DAVE, PSYCHICALLY, TO ME: "What the fuck is he talking about?"
> ME: "I'm sure he's getting to something cool. We just need to hang in there."

So we hung in there, waiting to see how this tied into something familiar. We knew Sean was giving us background — stuff that we had to understand but that would never appear in the story. We watched to see where he was going.

But after ten minutes, there was still no mention of dream extraction, dream police, mermaids, steam and clockwork, or anything else familiar.

> ME, PSYCHICALLY, TO DAVE: "If he'd at least give us a signpost. Something familiar. Anything at all. He was at yesterday's meeting, right? Maybe he suffered head trauma and has already forgotten everything that preceded today. Because none of this makes sense, given what came in Days One and Two."
> DAVE: "This meeting is like the finale of *Dexter*."

Sean told us about villagers who witnessed a nativity ceremony. There was a fork in the timeline, providing two possible futures. In one, a villager tried to steal the magic of creation from the terrestrials and celestials then failed. In the other, he succeeded.

Something about Stonehenge.

Something about Merlin, but somehow also Leonardo Da Vinci.

Something about King Arthur. And then at this point, Sean diverged into blathering about the golden age of Camelot.

We hung in for as long as we could, trying to be polite and not crap all over Sean's carefully conceived ideas, but ultimately we had to speak up. At the time, I think we might have felt underwhelmed by the ideas, but listening back recently I think we were merely caught off guard. The ideas are really interesting to me on a second listen, but they were *totally out of left field*. They weren't bad. They just weren't in any way, shape, or form — in any universe or fork in the possible futures laid out in the Akashic records — related to what we'd spent three and a half hours discussing thus far.

I felt a balloon deflating. The pressure of coming up with a story in a few days' time that would be worthy of writing under the gun had felt daunting from the start, and I'd felt like we were already a day behind due to Day Two bleeding into Day Three, but at least I'd felt energized by our Day Two ideas. At the end of the previous session, I'd felt a familiar species of what endocrinologist Hans Selye called eustress, or "good stress," feeling the clock ticking but knowing that the ideas were there and that we were well on our way.

But as the Day Three session unfurled and then soured, I felt like we'd got nowhere. We might as well still be on Day One, because we were no closer to a story. We'd simply wasted all that time, and now had to start anew. We'd gone around in a circle, juggling many disorderly ideas but honing in on none. We were back at the beginning, and I was supposed to start writing tomorrow. But how the hell could

I possibly put words on the page without another several days of intense planning?

The feeling that settled over all three of us was palpable. We wondered if the structure imposed upon us by *Fiction Unboxed* would prove disruptive after all. We'd up-ended our usual way of doing things, trying to jam too much into too small a space. We'd wanted to unbox our ideas, and instead felt trapped in a box. We'd never done any of this before. We'd also never required Sean to create his rough outline for a book — something we call "story beats" — so quickly. Sean's beats are usually comprehensive, including full character profiles, photographs or illustrations showing locations within our world, chapter-by-chapter outlines that I usually deviate from extensively but are at least there as touchstones when needed. That was a ton of work, and we were still days away, it felt, from even *beginning* that process.

What had we done? How could we possibly recover?

The only variable we could change — in a feeble attempt to restore a sense of closed-door familiarity from our usual process — was to allow Dave to leave and pretend we were alone, per Realm & Sands usual, with no audience, deadline, or pressure to perform.

I asked Sean what came next, feeling like the bottom had left my stomach. I almost wanted to cry with frustration. And the worst part was Sean looked and sounded the same way. When someone who's usually as ebullient as Sean is suddenly subdued and dour, you know that shit is slapping the fan.

We decided to break. To reconvene in an hour, after Sean took a short walk and tried to conjure a few simple story ideas. Fuck this "thinking too big" thing. We had to worry about story now, and a wider world later. We couldn't wrap our arms around the planet. We could embrace but one tiny corner. One snippet. A single seed. And if a forest was to grow, it could start there, at that seed, where it was meant to start — and maybe should have all along.

Day Three, Revisited

I spent that hour feeling about as bubbly as a stagnant pond. I lay on the couch. I talked to my wife, Robin. She said, "I'm sure you'll come up with a good story after a rest." But she was just saying that because she's my wife, and she loves me, and she didn't want me to think that I was in the middle of making a fool of myself in front of a live audience, which I felt certain I was.

Sean and I believe that ideas can come from anywhere. They are not few and far between; they are a dime a dozen. I've brainstormed ideas with groups of schoolchildren in five minutes that I could sit down and write novels about after a few weeks of noodling. In *Write. Publish. Repeat.* we said, "We don't believe in great ideas. We believe in taking any idea, and making something great."

But while that's true, we didn't have weeks to noodle ideas, to take our time and see where they went. We believed that the process could be accelerated — that we could do true improv, on the spot, if needed — but we'd never done so before. Story sessions fall flat; it's not smooth sailing all the time even for word machines like us. We knew that. Normally, when this sort of thing happens, we'll laugh it off and move on to the next project in our queue. Or if we absolutely must solve the current problem, we'll break for the day and sleep on it. But this time, we didn't have a next project. Or a day.

We reconvened after an hour had passed. I'm not much of a drinker, but podcast listeners (and Sean and Dave) make fun of me for drinking the occasional White Russian when the guys force me to do evening sessions. I never really "feel like I need a drink." On Day Three, I did. It was only 3:00, but I had one of the drinks *The Big Lebowski* made famous by my side when we started again.

Sean and I looked at each other like refugees. I think he asked me if I felt okay; I must've looked that bad. But we had to hash this out, and did.

We seriously considered trashing the first meeting's video. It was only our promise to "show everything" that made us decide to include it, and I'm so glad we did. In retrospect, *of course* we had to include that video, because it's important that "apprentice" writers understand that sometimes things go horribly wrong. Sometimes you feel like you've crashed and burned. But you haven't crashed and burned, or failed. *It's all part of the process.* When that happens you simply have to step back, take a deep breath, and try again.

And do you know who else needed to learn that lesson? *We* did.

Fiction Unboxed taught Sean and me a lot about our own process — things you'd think we'd know but didn't. We've ushered *Unboxed*'s lessons into future projects. Two of the most significant happened on Day Three.

First of all, **you must sometimes muscle past the suck if you want to reach the good stuff**. Never be afraid to stop, step back, and try again after some time away from the desk or page.

And second, **you have to do what works for you**. We knew we'd adjust our way of doing things for *Unboxed*, but ended up violating something too "core" to our process throughout Days One, Two, and the first half of Three.

Sean and I have always started small, taking a tiny spark of story and growing a world around it. It's part of how we work together. Even with *The Beam*, which Sean introduced me to via a ten thousand-plus word document full of timelines and background, I had a ton of false starts before I forced myself to forget most of it and focus instead on the micro-stories of the people highlighted by our tale.

We should have started with a story idea and built the world around it. And in the second meeting of Day Three, that's what we finally did.

(It's worth noting that Sean and Dave write together in the exact opposite way, which might have exacerbated *Unboxed's* problem. Dave outlines and world-builds very comprehensively, giving Sean extremely detailed story beats, whereas I want Sean to give me lean beats, knowing I'll fill out the details as I go.)

Relative to our day's first meeting, the events of the second were magical. Sean had come up with six, one-sentence ideas that were so frail as to almost be throwaways ("A society is divided into dreamers and builders"), but using them as seeds set us back on track. *Now* we were working as Realm & Sands usually worked. *Now* we were cooking with gas.

The first days' brainstorming wasn't wasted, of course. All six of Sean's ideas had come from that soup, tossing the terrestrials/celestials/Akashic records stuff out the window and focusing on things we'd liked from Days One and Two. In retrospect and despite my implications, I *do* actually think those meetings were needed — for Sean anyway. My presence, interestingly, might have been the problem. Usually, Sean percolates on ideas for weeks, but I don't typically see them until they're like the seeds he brought me on Day Three, part two. In other words, that banging around and mess of ideas always occurs ... but I usually don't see it.

We were on fire the minute we felt momentum. Sean had six sentences; we pared them down to the three we liked most and spent an hour fleshing out the concepts and adding meat to their bones. They were cribbed directly from the *Unboxed* site:

STORY IDEA #1: The people in our steampunk *LOTR* society are divided into two groups: dreamers and builders. The dreamers conceive ideas in their subconscious minds, and those ideas are passed on to builders to articulate and fashion. The two groups are separated and not allowed to intermingle. We have a "something is wrong and I don't know what it is" vibe in mind here, reminiscent of *Dark City* or *The Matrix.* We also want to introduce the idea of someone coming to realize she can be both things (dreamer and builder) and come into a latent power. There would probably be a disruptive "dream virus" used in this one.

STORY IDEA #2: Due to the influence of people outside the sequestered, walled-in society, our hero realizes that her dream world is actually real. This one would explore the line between fantasy and reality, and have a "freeing minds" vibe. One model we like for this one is the aesthetic of *Pan's Labyrinth*, though of course our story would be very, very different.

STORY IDEA #3: Sean used *Requiem for a Dream* as the vibe for this one. It would be about a "dreaming drug" that helps the society access deeper and deeper dreams, because the surface-level dreams are no longer cutting it. We think this would need to be the most adult of all three ideas.

There's a lot I like here, now that I know how the *Fiction Unboxed* story turns out. For one, although we put this trio of ideas to a vote (whichever our Unboxers liked best, we'd run with), the final story was actually a conglomeration of all three. That's because we're both "and" people and don't like to choose "or" if we can have it all. Secondly, all three story ideas mention movies as inspiration. We both think and write visually, and seeing how heavily we rely on visual inspiration has caused us to lean further and further into that tendency with every new project.

We didn't have characters yet, and we didn't have a plot. We didn't have a genre (we wanted to do young adult, but Idea #3 would make YA difficult), and didn't have even the barest inklings of an outline. I definitely couldn't start writing, and three full days were already gone.

But it didn't matter, because *this place was familiar*. Sean and I had been here before; it's where our story process usually starts. We were three days behind from my perspective, but I didn't care. I'd ended the first meeting deflated, and I ended the second elated.

We were on our way. We had the story's bones, and now all we needed was muscle.

Day Four

My son, Austin, had soccer practice on Tuesdays in June, and the practice at the end of Day Three, after my exhausting day of double meetings and emotional ups and downs, was particularly unwelcome. It was slated for an hour, so I dropped Austin off at the field and rushed to a nearby park to walk the path and clear my head. I had a half hour or so before needing to run back to pick him up, but as five minutes dragged into ten then into fifteen and thirty, I grew increasingly pissed. I could've kept walking. I didn't need all this overtime — and without a chair to sit in.

But as I stood there seething, I got a text from Sean letting me know that he'd just sent me some loose story beats via e-mail. We'd tied up our meeting a few hours earlier, so he must've got straight to work. I don't normally like to check my e-mail multiple times a day, but this was a special occasion. Besides, I had nothing better to do.

I sat down at the side of the soccer field, scrolling through a rather long e-mail from Sean. Eventually, I lay back and held the phone up above me, perusing what Sean termed "pre-beats" with a sense of magical fascination, like a kid reading a storybook late at night.

It was fascinating, how things had turned. That morning, we'd had nothing. That afternoon, we'd had less than nothing. By early evening, we'd had a spark. And there in my hands, I was holding a framework. My doubts disappeared. We still needed a day to find the story's finer points before I could start writing, but it would *only* take a day. We were now walking a well-worn path. We'd penned over two million words together by that point, and finally, with pre-beats in-hand, *this was something I knew we could do.*

I started Day Four elated, printing out Sean's pre-beats and filling them with chicken-scratch notes and questions to ask him about later during our sixth meeting in five days. My process here is a mess, but that's how it should be, because at this stage, Sean is the story's historian, and I am an archaeologist discovering the world centuries later. Rocks and bits of dirt fly everywhere as I prepare to quiz him, curious student to knowledgeable authority. (If you'd like to see this mess, by the way, we've linked to a picture of one of my marked-up pages on the resources page at SterlingAndStone.net/unboxedextras.)

Rather than recreating Sean's story outline, I'll include what he gave me below:

Fifteen-year-old Isla Steward goes to see a psychic. Her friend thinks it's bullshit, but Isla needs a solution — she thinks she's going crazy and doesn't know what to do. Isla has no idea what's happening to her. She's having dreams, but because no one in Waldron Gate dreams, she has no context for what that is and is afraid to say it out loud. It's as if she's living two lives. In one she lives in Waldron, as one of an elite class of citizens who work in the Ministry of Manifestation, in charge of bringing the impossible to life (with the help of the Blunderbuss). Isla gets some not-so-good news from the psychic; he tells her something that makes her look with a second eye around her, and listen to dreams that are hinting at a world that is richer than anything she could ever imagine.

In these dreams there is always a man, and because of something the psychic says, Isla — for the first time — listens to them, waiting to hear what he might say. But listening to her dreams has affected Isla's ability to manifest. As she's hooked to the Blunderbuss and trying to build, she slips into dreams. It goes from a rich fantasy world of popping color, slowly losing every pixel until it turns into this dingy, grimy — Darren Aronofsky steampunk — back alley steampunk on crack ghetto that looks entirely opposite of the Tim Burton + Suckerpunch of Waldron Gate. Standing in front of a giant, grimy cog is the man from her dreams. Isla wakes up and follows the memory to see where it goes.

Isla finds herself in the place where dreamers live. She meets Daw Blackburn, a dirty scientist who has been waiting to meet her for a long, long time. Daw lives "downstairs," with the man from her dreams, Levi Meade. They're two of the few to know the truth, that Waldron Gate is divided into two parts, and neither knows about the other. Isla is a third-generation Builder. This is as high as you can go without being in Parliament. Her job at the Ministry of Manifestation is to take some Crumble (she doses all day) and sit strapped to the Blunderbuss, where she somehow alchemizes thoughts into solid. The job of Daw's dreams department downstairs is to provide the Ministry with raw materials. The dreamers don't know that there are builders upstairs (or any upstairs at all). And as with dreamers and builders, every ministry upstairs has its downstairs opposite. Remainders and waste populate on the other side of the wall. This is also where Daw explains what dreams are. None of the scientists upstairs know the truth. They all think they're brilliant, running their ministries and creating something from nothing, but a few of the dirty scientists downstairs know the truth, and have been looking to Isla from below, pushing her to dream and meet them. Because, he says, Isla will change every-thing.

Isla is scared and wants to back out. She feels something in her gut, but doesn't know what it is. She doesn't understand empathy be-cause Waldron's upstairs warmth is so cold. She is somehow sorry for these people — and wants to get on Levi — but wants to get back upstairs. She's scared to think what might happen to her if anyone found out. She feels guilty for knowing what she shouldn't. Think how fucked up she would actually be, even though on the surface she would have anything she ever wanted. She would have to work hard to care, but Isla is also pure of heart, which is what makes her so pow-erful. She refuses, and gets back upstairs.

Isla is so upset that she has to take double her usual dose. When she wakes up dreamless, after having missed her shift at the Ministry, Isla realizes how hungry she is to dream. Her day on the Blunderbuss is awful. As she begins to build, she again starts to dream. But this time the dream shows her the horrible truth of what was detailed downstairs. She sees how it's like torture, as dreams are ripped from inside them. The worst are the waste management dreamers. Like precogs, they never leave their steam-driv-en prison. Most dreamers act as conduits, suck-ing all of the dreams from the people upstairs (both good and bad) then acting as a filter. The best ideas go upstairs, the indifferent and un-necessary are cast beyond the wall. Isla can't stand the torture. After her shift at the Ministry, she returns to find Daw.

Daw tells Isla that she must stop taking Crumble. Her dependency is numbing her gift. She is an exceptional dreamer, mayhap (lol for bringing mayhap to Blunderbuss) the best. Isla is outraged. She can't stop taking her Crumble. She's taken it every day since she learned how to swallow, with Crumble in her milk before that. She's been an hour off before, and it's horrible. Daw agrees with her: It will be horrible, but she has to do it anyway. Or all is lost. Isla agrees.

Isla goes home and for the first time ever, doesn't take her Crumble, allowing herself to fully dream. She is overwhelmed by the reality of it all, but because she's never fully dreamed her brain has no frame of reference to organize the information. Awesome for us, because we get to have a surreal chapter that's like steampunk *Lord of the Rings* with an S on its chest. Fantasy sequences in the book should veer sharply from Waldron's Gate. Total Guillermo Del Toro *Pan's Labryinth* aesthetic here.

Isla wakes up shocked to find a dream artifact in her hand and realizes that just as Morpheus, I mean Obi-Wan, I mean Daw Blackburn, prophesied, she is the first person in Waldron, and mayhap the world, to dream and manifest. She goes to meet the rest of the rebellion (including Coyote Sawyer!).

Daw leads Isla down into his hidden quarters. This area is BOSS because it's unlike any of the other settings so far. No builders ever try to dream (except for Isla), but some dreamers (those in the rebellion) try to build. The chambers are decorated with a few of their manifestations. In the chambers we hear the rebellion's plan for the first time, along with lots of quips from Coyote Sawyer, of course. They are all desperate to know what's on the other side of the wall. But they can only guess. They're constantly trying to contact the other side, but no one out there knows that they're trying to contact them, so it's like they're screaming into the forest instead of the city. They've invented some sort of boss steampunk technology that will bust down the wall, but they need to be sure of what's on the other side first. They can't tell fact from fiction in their minds. There are systems in place to keep them all from seeing the truth through their dreams, but Isla's Crumble is different from their drugs (theirs are like ayuhuasca: plant based and designed to blur reality) and she should be able to see it just fine, with practice. If all goes well, they will poison the system, bust down Waldron's wall, and change the world forever.

Awesome practice sequence where Isla is training inside her dreams. Yes, this is like *The Matrix*, but that doesn't mean it's not awesome. Let's just own it and make it our own. We do have to stick to one thing in this scene that *The Matrix* also does, which is show Isla's weakness. She needs to be fallible. Morpheus gets pummeled by Johnny Utah, but then Johnny can't make the jump.

Bonding scene with the rebels. More Coyote Sawyer.

Upstairs scene in Waldron Gate to show a contrast and now see the city with fresh eyes while Isla is getting itchy for Crumble.

She goes to sleep again without her Crumble, though this is a massive struggle. For the first time she experiences a nightmare, due to serious withdrawal kicking in. She wakes up and takes her Crumble.

She goes to the Ministry, manifests shit, then goes back downstairs. She has a sweet moment with Levi that's interrupted by Coyote Sawyer. She's terrified that someone is going to know she's back on Crumble. They go over the plan where she's going to poison the city's dreams. No one seems onto her. She leaves feeling guilty, but takes her Crumble once out of sight.

In her dreams, Isla fails. She has another nightmare, one with dragons circling the sky. She runs from the dream and somehow "leaves a door open" behind her.

Isla wakes up to an emergency in Waldron Gate — something that's never happened before. No one knows if it's true, but the rumor is that a dragon was shot down nearing the city walls. Chatter is everywhere. They don't dream, but Waldron Gate is rich in story. Legends of elves and dwarves and everything else exist in books that are celebrated throughout the city (it should be easy to love Waldron Gate if not looking at it with a critical eye). Everyone knows what a dragon is; they just can't believe there really was one in the sky. All they've ever heard about the outside world is that it's filled with "scavengers," a race of animal like people who feed on whatever they can find. Hence the wall's need to protect the Gate's citizens. Isla is A) desperate to get downstairs, but her disappearance would be too obvious and B) *not* take her Crumble, even though she is jonesing.

Isla finally gets downstairs. Daw knows what she did before she tells him. Levi looks disappointed, which cubes her *oh shit.* Daw explains what she did, and how she has to reverse it.

We drown Isla in her consequences. I won't know exactly what that means until after today's meeting, but basically this is an "all hope is lost unless she does everything exactly perfect" situation. The reader needs to understand just how hard this is going to be for Isla, body and mind.

Isla crushes it. This chapter takes us through her withdrawal.

Epic battle scene between fantasy and reality. The nature of this scene will be defined by today's discussion, but it should end with her coming inches from triumph and failing. By the final paragraph she must fall.

Isla is resurrected. We'll figure out how to do this today while we talk, but as long as it's not true love I'll be happy.

Isla's triumph, then final reveal: THIS IS HOW BIG THE WORLD IS ...

If you've read *The Dream Engine*, you'll probably notice a lot of things here that look familiar and some that aren't quite right. For one, our protagonist's name (pronounced EYE-luh) changed its spelling to Eila in the final book, and her last name changed from Steward to Doyle (after detouring briefly into Keally). Waldron Gate also became Waldron's Gate, plus a few other things.

But other than that, the book was definitely there in rough cut mere hours after a meeting in which we'd felt like all was lost. *That's* the magic of storytelling. Something can, if you keep at it, bloom from nothing at any time.

I asked Sean for details on everything. He continued to act as the authority, and I continued to query as if we were discussing a real place. Details settled into the middle as we sorted and sifted.

There are two key things to notice in this very rough story outline. The first is that these pre-beats do an astonishingly good job of hitting most of the finished book's main points. The beats are necessarily looser at the end (which changed quite a bit), but the signposts are there: Eila discovering the world under Waldron's's Gate, the horribleness of the Dreamers' plight, her accidental manifestation of the dragon, and her need to "battle" through the dark fantasy and break through to the other side.

But the second thing to notice (and again, this is easier if you've read the final book) is how much *isn't* here. Eila and her father's contrasting positions at the Ministry (her in Aether Forefront, the right-brained department, and him in left-brained Enigma) is missing, and that's a key turning point at the book's climax. We know nothing about what the machine actually is, what it truly does, where it came from, or what it means that Eila can Dream and Build. The existential, reality-bending nature of Eila's training sessions isn't in this summary, and that's a key point as well. In the end (and this is a pretty big spoiler), Eila doesn't need to learn the difference between imagination and reality; *she needs to learn that sometimes you can't be sure what's real and what's not, and that's okay.* She needs to learn, in essence, that in order to survive in a normal human world, you must be at least a little crazy. We don't see how Crumble works, what rituals surround it, the contents of Eila's neuroses and nightmares, I could go on and on.

Sean and I work like pencil and ink. It's almost as if he's taken a blank, three hundred-page book and written one sentence on every few pages ... and then it's my job to fill in the rest. When I joined Sean and Dave on the podcast, I told them that I literally didn't understand how two writers could ever write a book together, and if we worked the way Collective Inkwell collaborates, I'd maintain that position today. But for Realm & Sands, that's not how it is. Sean is much better at big ideas than I am, and he's said I'm much better at articulation of those ideas (along with discovery of fun things like theme and explanations for a book's occurrences and artifacts) than he is. It's a true partnership. Without Sean, our books wouldn't be as grand in concept and rich in color. And without me, they wouldn't have nearly as much depth and logical flow.

After the Day Four meeting, I felt like we were back on track — but not just on track; accelerating for sure. This was our sweet spot, where art and life flawlessly intersect over and over again in our work.

We were telling a story, and that tale was being told within the larger narrative of two writers crafting a novel live in front of an audience. Each informed the other. In real life, Sean and I can't decide between "or" ideas and always choose "and," so his summary encompassed *all three* of the proposed story ideas rather than sticking to one. He had referred to the untitled book as *Blunderbuss* for months, and now our novel's giant steampunk machine was called the Blunderbuss. We felt like we were living in the Matrix, and Matrix references (loose; you'll see one above) made their way into the narrative. Sean had failed at the beginning of Day Three to sell Dave and me on the idea of terrestrials and celestials combining to form "Crumble"... so guess what the drug in this version of the story was called? And perhaps most delightfully, during the Kickstarter campaign we'd used a social media blitzkrieg service called Thunderclap that did absolutely nothing for us ... so in the beats Sean gave me a few hours after the Day Four meeting (just two chapters' worth of more-detailed story; enough to start on Day Five), he created a ritual beverage called Thunderclap ... which, it turned out, did nothing.

We both had plenty of questions about the world, but after two million words written together, we know when to stop asking. There are things I need to know, mechanically, before I can write. And on the flip side, there are things I know I'll work out in the draft.

There's a difference between those two kinds of questions, and we're smart enough by now to see and respect it.

Answering the first kind of questions sets us out on the proper path.

But answering the second kind before discovering them along the way would spoil the most special surprises.

APPLY IT! This Chapter's Takeaways and Action Step

Here's the least you need to know from this chapter:
- You have to "work past the suck" sometimes if you want to reach your story's best ideas.

- You have to do what works for you. Don't let anyone else tell you how things "should be done." In our case, we messed with a system that worked for Sean and I by world building first, and paid the price on Day Three.
- The first phase of telling any story should be about generating ideas. No ideas are bad at their birth, but you must be able to quickly recognize something weak and have the perspective to toss it.
- True collaboration leaves little room for ego.
- The most complex ideas (*The Dream Engine* isn't exactly read on the short bus) can come from the simplest, single-sentence pitches.

And here's something you can do RIGHT NOW to apply this chapter's lessons:
- Come up with six simple pitches for a story set in a world you want to build. One sentence each, no overthinking. GO!

CHAPTER FIVE:
Beats and Hollow People

SEAN'S A FILM JUNKIE. HE'S always spouting filmmakers' names at Dave and me, looking like a pompous, artsy asshole as he prattles on about Darren Aronofsky's eye for composition or Paul Thomas Anderson's grand vision. He made us watch Shane Carruth's *Upstream Color*, then got all uppity when I was all *WTF?!?*. What a dick.

Sean's love of film has, without question, greatly influenced his writing and the style of our story architecture we've come to call beats. Beats used to refer to a very rough sort of outline (I described them in *Write. Publish. Repeat.* as "CliffsNotes written in advance by someone who wasn't paying much attention"), but they've evolved a lot since then. Now beats include not just story points, but other components as well ... all of which are spelled out using cinematic terms.

To provide a common frame of reference, we used to occasionally choose celebrities who would fit a given character, and in the beats Sean would say something like, "I'd cast Johnny Depp as this guy." But that tendency to cast the occasional character has blossomed into a complete casting roster, wherein Sean casts *every* major role and then gives me a full bio for each character, including a photo. He'll describe that character in detail, down to their history, their family, and any backstory that might influence who they are today. The combination of a real actor alongside a comprehensive fictional bio gives me a vivid hybrid feel for that person. (For example, someone played by Johnny Depp won't *be* Johnny Depp and would play the character as the character is written ... but in cinematic terms, Depp would of course "bring some of himself to the role.")

In addition to casting, Sean also routinely does "location scouting" for all Realm & Sands projects, pulling photos off of the Internet or fanciful art sites to pair with descriptions of that place so I can "see" it and "spend time in" it before writing about that place. By the time I get ass in seat to start telling our story, I typically feel like I know the place, the people, and all the dirty laundry inside it. I feel steeped and ready, so putting words on paper feels more like pouring water from a faucet.

But we had none of that as I began our still-untitled *Blunderbuss*. I had the roughest variety of beats, and the characters were nothing but names on a piece of paper. I knew that Eila was a Builder, and that Daw Blackburn was a scientist who lived underground. They were all hollow, their cores still in need of filling.

But the clock was ticking, so I started anyway.

Day Five

When my alarm went off at 5:45 a.m. on Day Five, I rolled out of bed, pulled on pajama pants, a shirt, and the same light-blue fleece I seem to always wear for a few minutes even on warm mornings. I put on my most common work footwear — a pair of dark-blue slippers that could probably be more manly. I started my coffee brewing, stepped into my office, and sat down, ready to begin, more excited than intimidated.

We'd untangled a few of the details between the lines of Sean's rougher-than-rough outline the previous day, already adding color to that first black-and-white etching and sowing seeds for what was to come. The drug, Crumble, became something that every topside citizen of Alterra took because not doing so brought insanity and got you shipped to the asylum. We'd decided that the Blunderbuss itself would have two halves — the top end only visible to Waldron's Gate, but the behemoth bottom plunging into dark and gritty Pavilion. We'd proposed the spark of an idea (mere background now, but it blossomed later): that the people of Alterra didn't truly understand what the Blunderbuss was or how to interpret what it allowed them to build, and that they were using it wrong. Even before the story's first word, I loved this aspect of our tale. If the engine gave Alterrans what they wanted most and what came easiest from their own citizenry's minds, its production would be linear and boxed in rather than truly inspired. They might think the Blunderbuss was doing the work of a god, but really it was scraping their psyches at the surface. It meant that rather than true creativity, it would simply continue to give them the whiz-bang versions of what they already had. If they had steam machines, it would give them bigger and faster steam machines. Why would the machine invent microchips? Alterra was a nation that had learned to think only as deep as their society required.

In my mind, the tendency of a steam-and-clockwork society to create more and more elaborate steam-and-clockwork machines rather than different kinds of machines gave our world *a reason for being steampunk*. Usually, steampunk is something a reader simply must accept: "In this world, there are big steam machines — got it?" But in this case, readers would see *why* it happens. This tendency to explain and delve and ask questions about the mundane is a hallmark of Sean's and my Realm & Sands imprint. Seeing it so early in this story gave me immense joy and excitement.

After our Day Four meeting, Sean had returned to the lab and written "1.0-type beats" (just text about the proposed plot, no further character or location work) for chapters one and two, fleshing out the story's beginning, and had them to me late that night. I'd read them before going to bed, and we'd batted a few questions back and forth by e-mail. I was ready to start and feeling more than capable when I stumbled into my office, morning coffee still gurgling through the grounds in the background.

I don't like to write before the coffee is finished because I'll only have to break in a few minutes to get a cup anyway. As I sat in my quiet, dark office, I looked down at my iPhone and decided that the morning was momentous enough to warrant recording a video while I was waiting. So I picked up the phone, held it at arm's length, selfie-style, and recorded a few-minute tour. (That video, if you'd care to see it, is at SterlingAndStone.net/unboxedextras along with our other resources.)

I finished the video, grabbed my coffee, and sat. I put on my headphones, then cranked my music loud enough to drown the world.

For a few minutes, I puzzled at the best way to begin. I knew I wanted Eila and her friend Cora to be at the solstice festival as our story opens, and knew the scene had multiple objectives. All first scenes should establish the setting, point to the characters' key problem as the narrative begins (in this case, the recent appearance of Eila's strange and terrifying mental visions), and give the reader enough tidbits about the people and world to interest them and, by dripping the required information, eliminate the necessity for an expository info dump later on.

In our specific example (while I was dropping hints about a dreamless steampunky world in which our main girl was suffering from nightmares), the scene's purpose was to get Eila to a psychic so she could have her troubling reading. Still, they weren't going to start at the psychic's tent. Great stories tease, and jumping right down the throat of the matter spoils the fun.

I looked at my screen, wondering. An opening should make a reader curious. It should hint at the stakes without giving too much away. It should leave a reader saying, "That was cool ... tell me more."

I thought: *They're at the festival. What would two teenagers be doing at a festival?*

Of course: *They'd be riding rides.*

Our story starts with a steampunk festival ride, all cogs, gears, steam, and clockwork. It was the perfect avatar for our genre, an ideal set piece to establish the world's tone. I imagined the ride, which I later named the Shuttle Shaker. I pictured the carnival barkers lining the midway, in black top hats. I thought of a mishmash of Victorian finery and black leather, of corsets and chokers and handlebar mustaches. And here's what came out:

> Toward the end of the midway, past the game barkers with their black top hats, culling the crowd for pigeons, past the tents of oddities and unlicensed innovations, was a great machine that had been unfolded from the backs of three flatcars on an East-West locomotive. Eila and Cora, who lived within walking distance of

the field that became the festival grounds at the solstice, had been watching its progress from parts to behemoth for days, in dribs and drabs as Eila's time off from the Ministry permitted. At first the machine had been nothing but struts and girders, pistons and clockwork. Slowly, as it was assembled, it had taken shape like something being born, growing and changing into a new vision with each visit. Today, as the girls stood before the machine's final form, it was like something terrible that Eila might have Built as it came to her off the Aether... or from one of her troublesome mental incursions. It stood a hundred feet tall, with giant gears and mechanisms that swung an armature from side to side, from up to down. With each cycle, a cloud of steam vented from a central boiler with a great hiss, as those strapped into it screamed for mercy.

That's the raw version, included here exactly as I wrote it that morning. By now, I've read the final paragraph dozens of times and listened to our audiobook narrator, Ray Chase, read it to me at least another five. It's barely changed. And that, to me, means that the world started right, its vision clear from word one.

From there, the opening of our tale spooled off almost as if someone was recording words for me. I saw Cora cowering in front of the ride and Eila goading her to get on. I saw the festival midway around them, then followed the friends as they backed away, and as Eila allowed Cora to recover her dignity. I got an immediate feel for their friendship — Eila superior in her social standing, yet more grounded and humbler than Cora, who came off as a high-society shopaholic teenager. The seeds of the scene's underpinning had already been planted: the *Ministry* and *Building* and Eila's "troublesome mental incursions." I needed only to follow. I described pieces of her nightmare visions as I saw them — all twisted and black like something conceived by filmmaker Guillermo del Toro. I trailed them to the psychic's tent, Eila pretending the errand was just for kicks — when, in fact, she truly wanted to hear what the Aether's other side had to tell her, and to find out if she was losing her mind.

I was clearing my throat; I knew that much of that first day was spent making false starts, overexplaining, and wasting words to find my way. It didn't matter. Your task is merely to begin in the beginning. And in spite of doubts, once you've begun, your task is to continue. You might not know all the answers, and will likely feel lost. But that's no reason not to start.

The day's words came slower than my usual pace, but all in all the effort was easy and natural, rapturously exciting. I was working in front of a thousand people (our Unboxers saw that day's raw words almost before Sean did, and saw later days' words *actually* before him), but I forgot that almost immediately.

There was the music.

There was the screen.

There was the keyboard beneath my fingers.

But mostly there was the story and the festival, Eila and Cora.

I was alone with them, oblivious to my watchers, in another world.

Day Six

By the end of Day Five, Sean had etched out the full book version of the story part of the beats. It didn't change much from that initial story summary, but he gave me what he thought of as logical chapter breaks and filled in some of the details we'd discussed. Of course, a lot of those chapters broke apart and rearranged almost on their own like a puzzle that refuses to obey its makers' cuts. Details churned through evolution, but we needed a place to start. And on the morning of Day Six, I had it.

Our beats were still rough and the story's characters hollow (I knew who a handful were, but not their fleshed-out backgrounds or quirks), so I mostly continued as I had the prior day, following Sean's signposts and making up what I needed as I went.

There's a great creative interplay in our collaborative relationship, and we refine it more with every project. Sean gets better and better at giving me information I'd rather have spelled out (how a character looks and acts, where she came from, and what she believes) and simultaneously gets better and better at *refraining* from giving me what I'd rather the story told me as I write it. I'm no stranger to working on skeletal beats; I just tended to flop and flail and clear my throat a bit more than usual as I found what I'm used to finding as well as what's usually spelled out.

The danger at this stage was that while I was free to create details on my own, Sean was also still furiously working on a full set of beats — and, in the process, creating details that contradicted mine. Our process usually involves a hand-off: Sean architects the story and outlines the characters, then I take that wireframe and smear it across the canvas until it all makes sense. This time, due to the time constraints, we were creating in tandem. It led to a few confusing moments (Sean clearly had something definite in mind for what the Ministry of Manifestation's "Pianoforte" event entailed, but I didn't know what it was and tripped over everything as I wrote), but we shrugged and said we knew it was part of our art. Soon, he'd catch up and we'd return to our groove. For now, I had to plow forward on my own.

On Day Five, I'd met Eila and Cora. On that day, I really only worried about Eila, because both of us thought that Cora would have no real impact on the story. (Spoiler: we were wrong.) So on Day Six, it was thrilling to reach the Ministry — to see the Blunderbuss rising from Alterra's bedrock, its enormous chrome-and-cogs girth pluming white smoke while Builders lay in their cradles on rings of scaffolding around it.

Throughout all of this, the story of the still-untitled novel (Sean referred to it as *Blunderbuss* as if that would be its final name) continued to intertwine with the larger, metastory of *Fiction Unboxed* itself. Neither of us believes that restrictions impair art; we believe instead that fences *define* the art, in the way a mold will define the shape of liquid metal poured into it.

So there we were, Sean scrambling to finish story beats and full character profiles while I stumbled through my own version of Alterra's Fog as words fell from my fingers. The constraints of *Unboxed* and our live viewership tightly wrapped the project, squeezing it into a distorted shape. We knew we needed to work with it, not fight against it. We built in pressure valves. The first time we see the Ministry of Manifestation, it's during the unusual Pianoforte event. Why? Because we didn't yet know what the Ministry was like, so showing it those first days during a time the reader understands is atypical bought us time to learn how things were supposed to work. We knew we wouldn't see the Ministry again for several more days ... and by then we'd know our newest world better.

In the beginning, because I didn't realize a blunderbuss was a real thing (an old rifle with a bell-shaped muzzle), I made the Ministry's engine capsule shaped. It was only later that we changed it, making the machine's ends belled to give *our* world's blunderbuss rifles a namesake.

In those first days, I needed to mention the wall around Alterra before Sean and I could discuss its logistics. I had questions about how a countrywide wall would work (How could it be truly impervious? Why would zeppelins never peek past it? Would nobody ever, *ever* try to climb it?), but because time constraints didn't allow me to check in, I changed it on the fly. If not for the rushed nature of the project, that wall might never have become the Fog — a far more intimidating and versatile zeitgeist foe for our characters, and a madman's playground in itself.

We pulled from *Fiction Unboxed* to stuff our fictional world. The machine had become the Blunderbuss, and our characters would drink Thunderclap. One of our Unboxers had referred to the scene in *The Matrix* where Neo fails his first trial — something we'd used for inspiration — as "Johnny Utah can't make the jump," and that phrase and story both ended up in the beats.

I kept my blinders on, trying to stay in the story world, but couldn't help but hear a few people rooting for us, encouraging us, waving flags and clapping hands.

I love praise. So I perked my ears for more, knowing it was a bad idea to peek out of my shell and hear what the outside world had to say.

And yeah, I was right. It was a terrible idea.

Day Seven

After three days and around twelve thousand words of raw draft writing, we held our first Q&A session for our live Unboxers. That session lasted nearly two hours, and we answered a lot of questions, but it began with a fifteen-minute diversion wherein Sean and I asked our viewers, listeners, and readers to help us help them — and to please not, through careless action, jeopardize the project for all of us.

Before commencing writing on Day Five, I'd made an announcement that I was sure would make me look like a prima donna: that until the draft was done, I'd completely ignore all e-mails, social media, blog comments, and forum threads having anything whatsoever to do with the in-progress story. I told people I'd practically vanish, that they'd hear from me again (save daily updates and meetings) when the story had been fully told. I left Sean holding the bag, instructing everyone to send their e-mails to him rather than me. I asked people to please not be offended if I didn't reply. I went hermit, underground, incommunicado.

My reason was simple: While a story is coming to life, it's as fragile as a newborn. It's the soufflé we've all seen in cartoons, where the slamming of a door ruins everything. Stories are wet clay, subject to shaping by any hand that cares to pinch it. The writer's mind must be fully his own. I wasn't supposed to be hearing *any* feedback — positive or negative — lest I find my internal compass turning in the wrong direction, or feel my confidence deflating like that soufflé.

And there I was, doing well, keeping my office door firmly closed, speaking only to Sean, asking my wife, Robin, to cull through my e-mail before I saw it and remove anything influential. But then I started to hear a few cheers, and listened harder. I checked my e-mail before Robin saw it. That was a mistake.

One hundred percent of the e-mail we got during Days Five through Seven had the very best of intentions, but that didn't stop some of it from being damaging. It all had the tone of, "I know I'm not supposed to say anything, but I just have one thing I need to say," ... *to save you from yourselves*, those e-mails' unspoken intent seemed to imply.

People told us we were leaning into clichés.

People told us that our characters seemed flat, and that our teens didn't speak like teens.

Even Dave — our collaborator, who loves us and gets us and wants only the best for us — sent us a very concerned e-mail detailing exactly what we were getting wrong without realizing it. *You are making fools of yourselves*, his e-mail seemed to whisper.

I once heard comedian Dom Irrera talk about "Italian eraser phrases," which allow people to say insulting things because the eraser phrase, which flanks the insult, undoes the damage, like: "That guy is a total lowlife piece of crap ... but I don't mean that in a bad way."

Dave's e-mail was like that, for me: *I want the best for you guys ... but you are screwing up so bad and don't even know it, and it's making you look like idiots.*

He actually said our Day One copy *made him cringe*. It was full of steampunk clichés. Our characters were cardboard cutouts. And so on. And so on.

As Sean and I began that Day Seven Q&A session, we asked — as kindly as we could manage — for everyone to *knock it the fuck off*. To say that those e-mails (even well intentioned) were demoralizing was an understatement. They were flat-out damaging. We were sharing first-days', raw-draft copy — the equivalent, for a writer, of standing in

Times Square naked. We didn't want or need critiques of material that new. Normally, the world doesn't see a writer's words until they've been shaped and sorted and poked and prodded and massaged and managed through the course of several comprehensive edits.

Our prose was unpolished, and our characters were flat? Of *course* it was! Of *course* they were! *It was the first mother-fucking day!*

I was calm by the time we held the Q&A, but I'd been furious when Dave's e-mail had come in. I knew where his heart was (and Dave, as you read this, know that I still do, but *holy shit, man,* don't ever do that again), but it changed nothing. I'd been mostly good; I hadn't read any forum threads, peeked at blog comments, watched social media, or solicited opinions. And yet we got those opinions anyway. It made me momentarily regret sharing our raw words. It justified every time a writer has refused to let an interested party read an early draft. "That's not ready yet," a concerned writer might say. Well, ours wasn't ready yet either.

I let Sean answer the e-mails, which he did and for which I'm grateful. I let Sean deal with Dave, because I was too pissed to answer him myself. And I insisted that we spend some time making it clear, in no uncertain terms, that undermining the confidence of the first-draft writer wasn't going to make for the best *Fiction Unboxed* experience. If anyone wanted to see us finish the book and get what they'd paid to see, Sean and I both needed to feel good about what we were writing *whether or not it was good.* Remember, writing *is* rewriting, and our subsequent passes would clear the wheat from the chaff.

We asked that everyone talk their hearts out among themselves ... but to please refrain, in all instances, from sending us story ideas.

The flood of well-meaning suggestions stopped immediately, because nobody had been trying to crap on us or our project, and everyone (and this is true of the wider *Self-Publishing Podcast* community as well as the subset of Unboxers) wanted what was best for us and the project. They'd truly been trying to help but hadn't realized how fragile this whole process was, and how even well-intentioned "help" could be the sand that clogged the gears of our great steampunk engine.

As the tide again turned firmly in the forward-facing direction, the engine rolled on into *Fiction Unboxed*'s second week — its cams and clockwork clear of debris, turning amid the clattering clanks of cogs, plumes of white steam billowing from its bell-shaped end.

APPLY IT! This Chapter's Takeaways and Action Step

Here's the least you need to know from this chapter:

- A well-told story is rarely clear in an author's head before it's started. It's fine to "clear your throat" in the first draft as you find your way, so long as you are willing to do the hard work of scrubbing your draft of all that throat-clearing later.
- Discovering your story as you go can be one of the purest joys of creation. Don't fear it. Revel in it.
- You have to ignore criticism while your door is still closed, even if it comes from the purest of places.

And here's something you can do RIGHT NOW to apply this chapter's lessons:

- Think of something you'd like to write, but that fear of criticism keeps you from starting. Something you know someone close to you would tear you to pieces for. Write that.

CHAPTER SIX:
Flow

DAY EIGHT WAS MY FOURTH day writing, and by then I'd got my blinders firmly back in place and mostly forgot the fact that so many people were watching. I wrote detailed blog posts for Unboxers to accompany each day's new words (and Sean was beginning to deliver edited, second-draft copy as well), but I did that with a different part of my brain. The part that woke each morning at 5:45 and wrote for a few hours in the morning's fertile soil felt all alone — or at least as alone as it usually was, with one collaborator and an always-supportive wife.

Most of all, I was finally starting to feel *normal*. The first week of *Fiction Unboxed* had felt stilted and odd, first with Dave joining our meetings (something we'd never done), followed by all that haphazard brainstorming and the falling apart on Day Three, then through the awkward first days of a fresh story, and finally with the confidence-busting round of well-meaning criticism. But that was behind us now, safely encapsulated in a completed Week #1.

(And in case you're wondering, *no*, I didn't hold any resentment whatsoever about Dave's e-mail or his saying our draft made him cringe. He's said that before about our stories, but usually waits until after they're published. Oh, and he says this stuff without actually reading our work, thus demonstrating his rather impressive osmosis skills.)

The dawning of the second week marked the start of our true period of flow. We'd altered our usual process somewhat to fit *Unboxed*'s time constraints (I was writing seven days instead of the usual five to churn out around thirty thousand words per week, and Sean was editing right behind me rather than waiting until the first draft was finished), but all in all it felt familiar. I'd shut my eyes and ears with new resolve; I focused on the story and listened to what it had to say. I sat in my chair with my keyboard on my lap, hitting the keys while a new world grew in front of my eyes. It was magical, like always.

Sean had finished casting our story, and I learned which actors would play the roles if our book were a movie, adding a new layer of familiarity as I told the tale. Eila would be played by Emma Watson. Eila's boss, Rabbit Brampton, would be played by John Slattery. Levi was Adrian Grenier, and Daw Blackburn (Pavilion's head dirty scientist and the leader of a group of revolutionaries known as the Guile) was portrayed (brilliantly, I thought) by Daniel Day-Lewis in a performance that recalled Bill the Butcher in *Gangs of New York*.

By the evening of Day Eight, Sean had nurtured that bare cast list out into a set of final beats, complete with character bios, photos and illustrations of people and machines and locations I needed to know, and a fully fleshed-out (through the first two-thirds, anyway) story outline. I knew I'd deviate from that outline significantly (Sean knew it too; that's why the final third was so scant), but the underpinnings were finally in place.

We were rolling.

Days Eight and Nine

I was rolling so well, in fact, that I kept telling Sean to take it easy, grab a beer, and kick back in a chair for a while.

Sean would text me, throughout Days 7 and 8 to say, "I should have final beats for you soon. Sorry it's taking so long!"

I'd say, "Dude, don't worry about it. I barely even need them."

I was trying to let Sean off the hook so he could get to some of the five million other things on his always-over-crowded plate, but it took the constraints of *Fiction Unboxed* — which evolved so much about our writing process for the better — to see that what I'd said was kind of like a girl telling her boyfriend, "These flowers are great, but you can pitch them because I already bought my own."

We joke a lot about how Dave, who worked with Sean for four years before Sean ever wrote with me, is Sean's wife — whereas I, who tend do be more adventurous in the projects I embrace, am the mistress. Jibes aside, there's a lot about a collaborative partnership that is like a marriage for one simple reason: A *relationship is a relationship*. Sean and I need to respect and please one another, and Dave and Sean must do the same. Dave and I have never written together, but we're partners in Sterling & Stone and on the podcasts as well as friends, so the same rules apply there, too.

In a relationship, each partner needs to contribute.

Each partner needs to receive.

Each partner needs to feel fulfilled, and happy.

And of course, communication is paramount.

I didn't understand a lot of the communication I was getting back from Sean about finishing the beats. I knew we needed to provide a finished set of beats to Unboxers, who might want to write in our story world, but that could wait. Right now, we had to get through the project. In my mind, given how good my writing felt, finishing those beats was secondary. Yes, they'd greatly enhance my understanding of the world and yes, they'd make the story better. *But we had too much to do and not enough time.* I kept trying to tell Sean that if fires were burning, he could let the beats go. "I have plenty for now," I continued to tell him.

And Sean kept promising to get them to me, saying that he really wanted to get them finished, that he was working hard, that they were important.

And I kept saying, "Don't worry about it."

But that was arrogant and stupid. This wasn't *my* story; this was *our* story. What I'd meant as a relieving of obligation was, in fact, robbing my partner of his creative input to the story and world. Beats are one of the things Sean loves to do. They take a lot of time to get right. He pores through the Internet for just the right photos; he crafts intricate backstories for characters with full knowledge that maybe 1 percent of that backstory will ever see the printed page. For this project, the completed beats contained a list of cities we barely mentioned, each complete with multiple, very cool steampunk illustrations. Once I got them, I knew all about Thestic, the Vatican City-like home to Alterra's prime church. I knew about the city of Stensue, which, like Sparta, was home to a military that I began to realize a country isolated by the Fog and without known enemies shouldn't have. And I knew about The Implement, a secret defense (or is it offense?) project that the Alterran government was covertly building, and which merited only a single passing mention in the draft.

I thought I was saying, "You don't have to do that." But what Sean heard, as I raced through the draft and built more and more of the world on my own, was "You don't *get* to do that."

Sean actually got me the finished beats on the evening of that second Sunday, before I realized how I was hogging the world building like a lone wolf. Thank God he did, and thank God I realized what was happening. The beats made our story. I was building in a single dimension. The detailed layers in those beats gave me the raw material I needed to branch out into three.

I devoured the beats, feeling like I was reading a AAA guidebook to the *Twilight Zone*. This wasn't a list of points for our story to hit; it was a rich repository of lore that I immediately began to salt into our narrative.

The people of our world believed in two gods: the Crown, who ruled the sky, and Jonah, a whale god who swam the ocean of Heaven beyond the Fog. Eila's mother, Juliette (a callback to Sean's idea to incorporate a *Romeo and Juliet* narrative, cast as Nicole Kidman), believed in the Crown, but her father, Atwell (Hugh Laurie), did not. Eila herself was undecided, but that made for a key character point when Eila, usually stoic, kneels down in front of the Pavilion door to pray to the Crown to maintain her sanity. And it told us something about Daw Blackburn that later we learn that he knew she did it ... and uses her moment of weakness as a weapon against her.

Starting on Day Nine, thanks to the seasoning made possible by Sean's full beats, our narrative moved from a good meal to an extraordinary one, from a fine steak to a table filled with expertly seasoned dishes. I'd had a paintbrush in hand already, but the beats gave me a palette of colors to work with.

I moved into Alterra, learning the names and emotions of those who lived inside it already. And with each day, knowing those streets and those motivations, I found new delightful relics and added them to the table.

Days Ten through Thirteen

But here's the thing about beats. No matter how great they are, they're only signposts. We'd set out in *Fiction Unboxed* to "demystify the art of storytelling," but that didn't mean we didn't believe the process held magic. There *is* magic there, but it's an accessible magic — one all of us, with practice and patience, can learn to find.

Working within the beats is, for me, a bit like driving one of those old-fashioned cars at an amusement park. Kids can drive them because even though it kind of looks like you're out tooling around on your own, there's a strip of metal down the middle of the track and if you try to steer too far in one direction, that guiding strip will always be there to nudge you back to center.

It would have been easy for us — for Sean especially — to hold off on starting our story until the beats were all finished. That way, we'd have had our fully fleshed-out guidance system in place. There would have been advantages, for sure. I would have known Alterra inside out from the get-go that way, from Waldron's Gate and its gritty Doer district in the south to rustic Yon up north. I wouldn't have had to guess at so many of the things I divined — so many of the things, truth be told, that we had to edit out or fix later.

But it also would have cost us four days. We couldn't afford four days, but for other authors "four days" is more symbolic than literal. Four days can sprawl into four months, and you'll end up telling your friends about these amazing plans you're crafting for the world of your story, and how you're *almost* ready to start … but not yet, because they're not perfect. All artists are excellent at finding reasons to postpone their art, and many of these reasons sound totally justified.

My beats aren't ready. I'm still thinking. I just need to figure out X. It'd be foolhardy to rush, right?

That's bullshit, and we know it. Chances are, you're scared. It's okay; we've been there. But you need to start. Over and over, we get questions on the *Self-Publishing Podcast* about details of our process that we've shared as (you guessed it) part of *our* process rather than advice for everyone, but that someone has latched onto as gospel. People ask us all the time about what format beats should follow, how long serial episodes should be, whether three novellas at twenty thousand words is a better product line than two at thirty thousand. The answer — and yes, this is also true of the new beats process we love so much — is that our process is our process and works for us … but that your process may differ. Listen to us, but listen to yourself more. Listen to yourself, not the voice of resistance and doubt. Listen to yourself, not the voice of procrastination. And when in doubt, *get started.*

There was a lot of magic interplay during the first part of the novel, where the pre-beats informed the work, and the work informed the beats. Sean added the idea of the Fog to the beats after I'd discovered it in writing *without* them, and the Fog became a central part of the story. His beats went on to explain the differences in the Fog at different points around Alterra: e.g., if fanciful lore is believed more fully outside of Waldron's Gate, where the mental callus of dream-siphoning is thinner, wouldn't the Fog's contents at that area be closer to the everyday reality — where, by the way, they'd naturally have fewer goods manifested by the

Blunderbuss and hence need to tinker with their hands to create what they needed ... and hence exercise their minds more than Waldrons' citizens ... and hence, maybe, *dream* a bit beyond what Crumble could steal?

Once I began working with the beats, that interplay didn't depart. It simply changed forms. The best beats are merely markers beside a long and winding path, there to nudge the writer back on track if he strays too far. If I went off on a tangent to explain some aspect of our world (this happens often; I'm an explainer by nature), I'd still always have one eye on the beats and know how I needed to turn it around to hit my next marker. But between the intermittent signposts the beats gave me, the meandering was frequent and amazing.

The story evolved, beats and draft bouncing off one another day by day. I stretched some of Sean's single-sentence mentions into full scenes and collapsed entire chapters into a scattering of paragraphs. I explored the nature of Eila's relationship with her father (which the beats had nailed) and with her mother (which was quite a bit deeper and more complex than the beats had imagined). I created new, ancillary characters as I needed them (like Al, a kindly workman from the Doer district who guides Eila to the waste machine we named the Convenience on that first visit, allowing her to then manifest the doorway she follows to the underground city of Pavilion, where the Dreamers labor) and discovered hidden bits of lore along the way. Wouldn't the poor people of the Doer district need to build and scavenge more than the upper class of downtown? And what of the people of Pavilion? What would it take for none of them to question a world with no sky, bounded by walls made of rock?

Eila found her way down through the convenience. She wondered what I wondered, and I found Levi and our dirty scientist Daw providing the answers. The answers begat more questions, some beginning to smell distinctly thematic: If the people of Pavilion, after a thousand years underground, accepted their enormous cave as how the world is, what did that say about Eila, who was topside and free, but whose world was bounded by a Fog they did not question? And more globally: What did it say about us, here in the real world, reading the story on Earth? Were we as free as we believed? Eila was questioning her mind, the refrain of "sanity is a matter of opinion" surfacing like a fossil. So what made *me*, in my chair in my quiet office, so sure I wasn't suffering from my own brand of insanity?

Eila had a long conversation with Daw, who explained the dual-ended nature of the Blunderbuss as Sean and I had decided it. Daw spoke for us, telling the reader how the world worked. Eila asked questions that I didn't know the answers to, and Daw, obliging fellow that he is, answered them under my moving fingers.

I began to see seeds of background that wouldn't make it into this book but that would matter in later books. Eila's father had trained Eila to ask disruptive questions. Why? Did he know more than we thought, and would his rebellious nature manifest in plots later on? Her mother, Juliette, had done the same, taking her to the Fog's border at age eleven so she could gaze into it and "know the nature of the trap that surrounds her." Why? We'd thought Juliette was merely a *Stepford Wives* authority at the Ministry of Decorum, but there was clearly more below the surface. Phoebe Horn, of the Guile, was a talented Pavilion Dreamer whose psyche was so twisted that her nightmares soured Dream shifts for the others on the array with her. What had made her that way?

Things began to feel easy. The draft wasn't yet one-third complete, but given the front loading of all that uncertain brainstorming time, the overall effort was past the halfway point. And the metastory — the story of the entire *Fiction Unboxed* project, where two crazy authors rally their community and then write a book live — was almost in the homestretch after all the prep and Kickstarting. We were cruising.

On Day Ten, we had another meeting. We discussed the cover, knowing we had to give our designer, Erin Mehlos (who'd done the amazing *Unicorn Western* cover the prior year), something to work with. We decided we wanted Eila on the cover alongside our great chrome machine. Our part was simple, and we trusted Erin to give us what we needed.

Far harder was Day Ten's title discussion. We wanted something that sounded steampunky, something that worked for a young adult reader, and something that managed to pique attention while not putting those curious people off by being *too* weird.

It's funny how things always come around, and it's funny, in retrospect, to see how they start.

We didn't decide on our book's title for sure for nearly another week, but only on a recent re-listen did I notice something I said in that Day Ten meeting as a throwaway line — something that could have been said in a whisper, for all the attention we gave it.

"What do you think about something like *The Dream Machine*?" I asked. I paused. "Or The Dream *Engine*?"

APPLY IT! This Chapter's Takeaways and Action Step

Here's the least you need to know from this chapter:

- Creating "beats" before starting a story will help you to go faster and will keep you writing.

- But ... beats are *only a guideline* and they should never enslave you. Deviate all you want, returning to the center only to hit those signposts your story must find ways to hit.

- You should always be enthusiastic about your work even if you think it's sloppy. You can always clean it later.

And here's something you can do RIGHT NOW to apply this chapter's lessons:

- Write one page of beats for a short story, or a few thousand words worth for a novel. Don't overthink it. Just give the high points about what might happen.

CHAPTER SEVEN:
Finding Fossils

THERE ARE TWO MAIN WAYS that Sean and I write together.

The default is for me to compose the first draft, then for Sean to edit once and polish once before sending the draft on to our editor. In that default arrangement, I won't see a project again until after it's been published.

But for certain highly complex projects, the flow goes me > Sean > me again. The *Unicorn Western* series is this way, as is *The Beam*. For those tricky, lore-rich stories, we like to get an additional pass just to make sure our vision is fully articulated and all of the cross-references (and story lore) make sense. It's a huge time-spend, and we wouldn't have had time for it on *The Dream Engine* even if it had required it.

Unfortunately, I did require it.

And unfortunately, we had to find a way to make it work.

Stephen King makes an amazingly apt metaphor in his must-read book on writing titled (wait for it) *On Writing*. He says that stories aren't created by authors; they are things that are buried in the ground, existing in full as the story-teller discovers their edges. An author's job, therefore, isn't to *create* a story. It's her job to *discover* it.

In our experience, this is 100 percent true. It's delight-ful, because it means we get to be as surprised unearthing our stories as the reader. But it's also a problem, because it means you don't always know in advance what you're going to get. Yes, you can work within constraints, and yes, you can usually guess how much space and time a given story will tell. But sometimes the story pushes back, and demands more due. We'd seen it with *The Beam*, which screwed up our 2013 calendar by demanding twice the length we'd allowed, and we were seeing it now, during *Fiction Unboxed*, when time was already at a premium.

We could have ignored what the tale was telling us, but we consider ourselves to be caretakers of stories, and hence must always do what is best for them.

So we dug in.

Sean was already editing right behind my new words, and he'd begun looping back and doing his second edit (which he calls a "polish"; it's about shining up salient story facets and making them glow) in tandem. This created a strange sort of vertigo; he had trouble remembering what came first, what had been foreshadowed and what hadn't. It meant that we'd be able to do all that needed to be done in time — that I'd have words that had been edited, polished, and proofread by our editor in barely enough time to do my own final polish — but it meant a lot of overtime.

It didn't matter. The clock was ticking, and Eila's tale deserved our very best.

We kept writing, discovering more every single day as our audience held their breath, cheered (some cheers made it through my self-imposed isolation), and were unable to contain their excitement when we met them in Q&A sessions.

Fiction Unboxed's story arc was rising — and of course, as in any good tale, that meant a crisis was coming.

We should have known enough about story to see what was waiting for us on Day Twenty, but for some reason we didn't, assuming that smooth seas would stay glassy.

And so until the dam cracked, we were content to keep digging.

Days Fourteen and Fifteen

Remember that initial criticism, where people said our characters were flat and they didn't sound their age? That happened because at the beginning of any project (and by that, I mean the beginning of writing, not necessarily the first pages), the characters *are* flat. We've learned to shorten our characters' learning curves a lot with a more fleshed-out beats-writing process, but there's always a time when you don't know these people well enough to articulate what they'll say, what they'll do, and how they'll act.

But there's more than just a writer's unfamiliarity at work in those first bits of story. Chronologically, at a story's true dawn, most characters are merely shadows of who they will become by the tale's end. Great characters grow and evolve as the writer is getting to know them. In any well-told story, a reader should feel closer and closer to characters as time passes — as they acquire depth and history and as that alchemy engenders empathy ... or hatred.

As our story approached its midpoint, Eila became more and more of a true person. We finally met her family, and with them as foils we got to know her better. In the beginning, Eila acted like a little adult: young but somewhat stiff. And that was fine, because Waldron's Gate is a somewhat emotionally stunted place thanks to the theft of its citizens' dreams. But when Eila goes home and we see her interact with her people, we see that she's like any girl: protective of her younger sisters, snippy with her annoying brother, a bit distant from her mother (whom she's not so much like) and close with her father (whose temperament she shares).

We saw in Days 14 and 15 that our heroine isn't always so self-assured, that she wants to please her parents while trying to forge her own identity apart from them (a battle that every teenager tries to wage through varying degrees of futility; "I'm not like you" often succumbs to the twin forces of genetics and life experience), that she doesn't yet know who she truly is, that she's always been certain of her position in the world and now faces a crisis as its challenged.

On Day Fourteen, I gave Eila a truly harrowing experience — one I felt myself pulling back from versus how I'd handle it in a more adult novel. During a shift at the Ministry, her wondering, prodigious mind detaches and follows a thought backward through the Blunderbuss until she encounters the Dreamer who sorted the dream before it came upstairs for the Builders to manifest. She sees how the Dreamer is besieged by horrors daily, and what toll the weight of an entire nation's nightmares has upon a mind that was built to handle only its own. The experience leaves Eila scarred. She realizes how much she is part of the problem and finds herself unable to unsee what she's seen.

Eila begins to understand the true cost of the Ministry's actions. By continuing to Build the ideas that come through the Blunderbuss, she is now a willing exploiter and torturer of the Dreamers below.

In pretty much any good story, the flow goes like this: a character is complacent; she faces a conflict; she adapts; she grows.

We'd made it that far, and both Eila's strengths and her seams were beginning to show.

She knew what was wrong, and she knew that she had to make a decision.

We knew what we wanted that decision to be, but as I've said, stories are fossils, and characters are their own people. A writer cannot force his will upon a story. He must listen to what the story and its characters tell him.

We knew Eila had to face her fears, to own up to her responsibilities and do the right thing.

But she fought so much harder against us than we'd anticipated.

Days Sixteen and Seventeen

Throughout all of creation, there are two primary forces at work: *entropy* and *order.*

The universe always embraces entropy, striving to equalize inequalities, to iron out knots and wrinkles, to turn all that exists into an undifferentiated average where all matter and energy is perfectly distributed across all that exists.

But on the flip side, life strives for order, expending great amounts of effort and energy to make it happen. Bodies build defenses like shells and skin. Life forms congregate in groups, attempting to pool their experience, protection, and knowledge. As the world ravages populations, life forms mass produce more of them. Evolution has created better nervous systems, stepping from isolated reflex pathways to ganglia to brain stems and cerebella to the big, wrinkled brains humanity has today.

On a primitive, unassailable level, people will always strive against being changed, because passive change means entropy. A body wants to maintain its own borders. It wants to determine its own fate. And so when outside forces assail characters who are otherwise complacent, their first instincts will always be to flinch back. To keep things as they are, where the boat doesn't rock. That's deep-down, monkey-brain stuff. That's homeostasis: a bones-deep resistance to change what might result in a threat.

It would have been simple for us to write Eila as accepting of her duty, but it would have been a lie. It would also have been thematically inconsistent, because one of the biggest things *The Dream Engine* was telling us was that the world holds few objectively right or even real things. We knew that as a human being whose deep brain strove for order, Eila would be quite capable — willing and willful, even — to both know the Ministry was wrong and refuse to leave it. We knew that Eila would, in all likelihood, choose to feel guilty for what she'd seen of the Dreamers' plight before she'd choose to act on that guilt and initiate change.

She'd been raised to be a Builder. Her father was second in line at the Ministry, and had worked hard for what he had. Everything in Eila's society was based around Building and manifestation, and that delicate balance teetered on what she now saw as torture. Yes, it was wrong. And no, she couldn't bring herself to change it, or even leave it. She was a character in our story, yes. But Eila was also human.

The turning point in her arc came when we sent Eila back down to Pavilion and Daw tells her that her torment is coming from her refusal to embrace what she must do.

She must learn to fully Dream, so she can Build them a way past the Fog.

But in order to do that — in order to integrate her troubled mind and resolve her dilemma — she must go off the drug that all of Alterra takes many times daily. The drug — she believes, knows, and feels — that keeps her sane.

There was a lot of lore here, and we had to work hard to make an entire nation's dependency on Crumble realistic. It meant deviating from Sean's beats quite a bit, telling more tales and giving more history, and having Eila spend a lot of time in fractured-mentality introspection. She had to grow to believe that as painful as going off Crumble was — as sure as she was that it would land her in the Joffrey Columns asylum, where a disturbing bevy of steampunk-style psychiatric treatments awaited — staying on it was actually *more* painful.

This was the part of the tale where we knew we had to twist the knife in our heroine's gut for her own good. So when she heads back down to Pavilion, her second scene with Daw Blackburn had to hurt. She had to see her role in Waldron's abuses. She had to see (via a fight scene with Cora before she headed down) that she's changed and no longer fits her old world. She had to see that she couldn't go back if she wanted. She had to feel the pain of lying to her parents, of keeping a false face at work. She had to envision what life would be like going forward if she refused to quit Crumble. Did she expect to keep putting in shifts on the Blunderbuss? Did she expect to keep causing torment below, and continue the lies to her father?

One of the things I like most about Eila's second conversation with Daw is how it reinforces the uncertainty inherent in her coming journey — and, by reflection, in our world at large. We can never know what will happen; we can never know if we are correct; we can never be sure that how we see the world is as it truly exists; we can never know that all will be well, even if we do everything right.

Eila begs Daw for solace, but she's no longer a child who can count on the false assurances parents give when children are still young and foolish enough to believe them.

The scene ends like this:

"If I stop taking Crumble," she said, "what will it be like?"

"It will be hard. Then you will adjust, and it will be like opening eyes you didn't realize had been closed."

"And then I'll feel good again. Normal, like all is all right. Like everything will be okay."

Daw shook his head. "All will not be okay."

"You said I'd adjust."

"You will adjust to how it will become, not how it was."

She sniffed again, refusing to snatch her hand back to wipe her eyes. "Just tell me I'll be fine. When it's all said and done, tell me that I'll be fine."

Daw continued to slowly shake his head.

"I can promise only two things," he said. "The first is that everything will be different. Not good, but not bad either. *Different.*"

"And?"

"And I can promise that you, Miss Doyle," he said, "are our only chance."

We don't always want to bear what we must in life, and can never know that everything will be okay no matter how much we want it to be.

Our little girl was growing up — whether she wanted to or not.

Days Eighteen and Nineteen

When I was first transitioning to writing full-time, I recalled something that Stephen King (yes, him again) said about his work habits: He works to heavy rock music, played loud in order to drown out the outside world. At the time, this was as intriguing as it was highly unrealistic. I work at home, and we homeschool our kids. That means they're around often, and that my office is seldom the quiet haven that Sean's sometimes is. Working to music would be a great solution ... but how?

I used to find the idea of writing (which involves words) while listening to lyrical music (which also involves words) impossible to conceive of. Today that's how I write all my fiction: wearing large, over-the-ear, stereophonic headphones. I taught myself to do it, and I'm still not sure how. But I suspect it has something to do with my writer's trance.

I don't know how it is for most writers, but I'm barely present while telling my stories. I don't feel so much like I'm creating something as I'm watching and listening very closely to see what happens. A different part of my brain sees the action unfolding as hears the music, and a different part of something else entirely is in charge when I'm following a character's unpredictable actions — something that happens a lot during all stories, but which happened even more than usual while writing *The Dream Engine*.

You could ask me where some of the turns came from in what followed, but the truth is that I don't know.

When Eila came home in Crumble withdrawal and began to see something moving under the butter dish, that didn't come from the beats. Even "Eila freaks out at dinner" wasn't in the beats ... nor was dinner.

When Atwell pulled his daughter aside and implied that he knew she was suffering from something — even spouting a phrase out of the blue to name it: "depth syndrome," which is like diver's narcosis for Builders who go too deep and lose track of what's real and what's not — it didn't come from my own conscious choice.

When it became clear that Atwell knew Eila was lying to him, it surprised me. We hadn't planned for that or discussed it. It simply occurred.

And when Eila skillfully deflected her father's interrogation by blaming her distraction on "girl stuff" — something any father would back away from with his palms raised in surrender — I was as pleased and disarmed as any reader.

So let's get that out in the open: *We, as the writers, don't know what's going to happen next.* We have general ideas, and we have plans, but they seldom work out exactly as we figure, and the details of how they unfold are as much of a mystery to us as to anyone.

Your job as an author is to give your story the most fertile ground you can in which to grow. Water it. Listen to it. Obey its needs. Have a plan and nudge where you're able, but always go where the characters and the story want you to.

So there I was, puttering along through Sean's beats and listening to where Eila wanted to go. She was distraught and unhinged when she came home, but I knew she was strong and resourceful, that she'd make it through the night despite her overwhelming fear. And I as the writer knew something that I couldn't assure her about and that Daw (that jerk) didn't bother to fully articulate — probably because she was supposed to learn it for herself.

A mind that's free to dream is untidy, and horrors intermingle naturally with delights. Every person doubts herself. Every person sees metaphorical shadows in the gutters; every person looks in the mirror sometimes and wonders if their own perception of themselves is true. Every person has monsters in their closet and under their bed, and every one of us must sometimes deal with doubt.

We know something that Eila, her first night off Crumble, couldn't know: that although we all feel uneasy and afraid from time to time, those feelings are all normal.

A mind off Crumble is a messy thing, and living with one means being okay with being just a little crazy.

I watched Eila go to sleep amid her doubts.

I watched her travel a nightmare dreamscape, my writer's mind delighted with the fantastic sense of play that journey provided.

She entered the Fog, exploring a world that was clearly unreal, clearly more *Lord of the Rings* than the steampunk we'd seen thus far, populated by stories she and all of Alterra knew from its collective lore.

And from that unreal world, via her undrugged sleep, Eila manifested a relic she found in her bed upon waking.

The fantasy world, it seemed, could be plenty real, under the manipulations of the right mind.

That meant that our story had its stakes; all we had to do was to deliver on them.

If, that was, we had enough faith to get through the four calamities in five days that we didn't know were waiting.

APPLY IT! This Chapter's Takeaways and Action Step

Here's the least you need to know from this chapter:

- Your story is alive if you listen to its whispers ... so listen!
- Writing is rewriting, and you should never worry about getting things perfect the first time through. One of our favorite expressions is "Perfect is the enemy of done." Be "done" rather than perfect.
- Your fiction-writing process can and *should* be tweaked as you constantly develop as a writer.

And here's something you can do RIGHT NOW to apply this chapter's lessons:

- Based on what you've written so far, detail three ways you know you could improve your process right now. (**HINT:** Don't be afraid to fix what isn't broken. Improvement, even of something that's already good, is *always* possible.)

CHAPTER EIGHT:
Emergency!

IN THE FIRST SEASON OF the TV show *LOST*, the big question was what exactly lurked within the mysterious hatch that Locke and Boone found on the island. It took them about half the season to find that hatch, then viewers watched with baited breath for the rest of the year to see what might be inside.

Most people don't realize that the contents of the hatch — which shaped the entire rest of the series — was *unknown to the show's creators* when the first season ended. They needed a mystery, so they made a hatch. They didn't worry about the details to follow, such as "What the hell is this thing?" They just stuck it in the ground, unsure, and figured that they could work it out in Season 2.

Sean and I are both, as of the time we're writing this book, re-watching the entire *LOST* series from start to finish. We weren't writing for a living when we saw it the first time. Now we are. And because of that, we can now snoop below the surface, imagining what those writers must have been thinking and feeling, because we've done the same things ourselves. Over and over, we'll reach the end of one book's story arc without knowing what will happen in the sequel. When that happens, we'll simply "make a hatch" and hold our breath, knowing we'll have the time between books to figure out what we've done.

It's a neat concept, but you may be wondering what Dave wonders about this kind of thing: *what if you write yourself into a corner?*

Our answer — and this satisfies Dave not a whit — is that we don't believe it's *possible* to write yourself into a corner so long as you're honest, listen to the story, and diligently excavate the fossil.

Because every story comes out somewhere. This is especially true if you believe that the story is there for you to *discover* more than *create*. So Sean and I make our hatches. We hold our breath and cross our fingers, then release our stories into the world with no idea how the hell we'll escape from Houdini's box when it comes time to write the next one. And so far, we always have.

This takes faith. That can be a strange concept for a writer, but it's something I've seen dozens of times. It used to bother me. I used to think, "I have no idea if this story will come together." The book we wrote after *The Dream Engine* (a mindbender of a novel called *Axis of Aaron*) tested us more than anything we've written so far. It's nature is to bend reality, to leave the reader guessing which end is up. Sean and I felt like two guys rowing a dinghy through the middle of high seas throughout the process, praying we ended up finding shore. But we did. Because an honest storyteller, given enough practice, always does.

But we didn't have *Axis* under our belts as *Fiction Unboxed* entered its final week, and although our faith was strong it wasn't yet bulletproof.

Given that we had a live audience of a thousand people watching our every move, it's lucky that we managed to untie all our story's complicated knots before hanging ourselves.

Day Twenty

The first of our four unscheduled meetings in four days — and, of the four, the least dire — came on Day Twenty. I was tooling along that morning when I realized three things from nowhere:

First, although I'd plowed through a huge number of rough draft words and felt like I was on pace, there were still a lot of events left in Sean's story beats that I'd yet to cover. That was a problem, because this was the end of Day Twenty's writing, and I'd hoped to be done with the draft around Day Twenty-three. But it wasn't merely the ticking *Fiction Unboxed* clock that bothered me about the pacing; I knew this was the first novel in a new young adult series and that going too long, regardless of the reason, would be a mistake. *The Hunger Games* is one hundred thousand words, *Twilight* is 120,000, and *Divergent* is 105,000. You should never write to a formula ("YA books of this length sell best, so write one that long"), but you *should* write for your reader. If we went too long, we'd be in danger of boring our target market — and we already have a tendency to be verbose.

Second — and this something about this had bothered me since the first set of finished beats — there was a lot of back and forth in what I had left. We'd already sent Eila down to Daw twice, and Sean had her yo-yo'ing up and down a few more times yet. Eila was supposed to go to Pavilion, do X, return upstairs, and do Y ... then repeat. She went up, she went down. And yes, life is full of cycles, so I couldn't put a finger on why it bothered me, but it did. It was beginning to feel like a mundane diary: "Dear journal. Today I got up, brushed my teeth, and went to Pavilion again. Then I came home to dinner. Again." We needed to crack that rhythm and find a way to make the required events happen without recounting all of Eila's comings and goings.

And third, I'd been walking my talk, listening to the whisper of the characters and the story as they told me what to do — and that morning they'd told me to have Eila run into her old Waldron's Gate friend, Cora, again. I wasn't sure why this had happened; I hadn't seen it coming, and it wasn't in the beats. But it felt right. Eila had been told to go off Crumble; she'd started to freak out; she'd woken the next day and practically overdosed as a counter-reaction and run to find Cora. That wasn't the way Sean had planned it, but it was what Eila wanted to do. So she did it. But, as is true for the parent of any teenager with a mind of her own, I wasn't sure why Eila was doing what she was doing or what might happen next. She'd already met with Cora once after discovering Pavilion, when Cora showed up outside the Ministry. That encounter had ended badly, with Eila blowing her off. Even though *Eila* had gone to *Cora* this time, I didn't see how this new scene wouldn't just repeat the previous scene's argument. We were in danger of looping, of repeating ourselves.

I called a story meeting for that afternoon. Because Sean was editing right behind me, he was mostly caught up — a rather nice benefit for untying story knots that we've since incorporated as part of our regular writing process. He read that morning's words, and we began to untangle the knot.

Sean thought it made sense to start with the Cora scene, so we did. We asked: Why did Eila go to Cora? What would Cora feel about it all? Eila needed to get back down to Daw and begin the training that would help the Guile cross the Fog. So was she supposed to take Cora with her? And if so, what good would it do for the story?

We pitched the last idea immediately. If Cora went down, we'd need to write a discovery scene. We'd then need something for Cora to do in Pavilion, would need to weave her own web of lies, and so on. It seemed to make the most sense for them to fight. Because, we realized, she'd want to. Eila had snubbed Cora earlier (Eila had left Cora feeling that Eila, a prestigious Builder, was too good for her), and her best friend would still be angry. Eila had OD'd on Crumble because she was terrified of a nightmare, but neither the overdose nor running to Cora had been rational acts. Both had been Eila trying, yet again, to restore order and turn her back on what she must do. She'd reached out to the familiar — not to repair their friendship for Cora's sake, but to cling to her last shreds of normality like detritus bobbing on the water beside a sinking ship.

They had to fight, and the fight had to serve the story. But what about?

As the scene stood, I'd had Eila start to explain her secrets to Cora. As with their meeting, I didn't know why or where it was going, but we followed that trail. Eila should keep explaining, but Cora shouldn't believe her and become angry at the deception. Or ...

There was a spark. At this point, Sean held up his arms and said, "NO, wait. I know ... THIS IS *IT!* THIS IS *IT!*"

The fight would be about Levi, Eila's teen guide who'd summoned her in the first place.

It made perfect sense; Cora was the perfect boy-crazy foil. Eila would broach the idea of Pavilion by leading with a topic that interested Cora — a hunky teen guy — but then something would go wrong. They had to fight, and the fight had to feel like a betrayal.

Cora had to recognize Levi, and she had to think that Eila, with her Builder's mind powers, had been snooping in her head.

We had to make Cora a sketcher, and write an end-of-chapter reveal wherein Eila realizes that the guy she's described happens to be all over the sketchbook Cora carries with her everywhere, as if Cora has been (wait for it) *dreaming* of Levi.

And sure, it was true that thus far, Cora didn't carry a sketchbook, but that was easy enough to fix. We'd simply "salt" the idea throughout on the polish, adding mentions here and there of Cora and her sketchbook, so that the reader, at the moment of the reveal, would say, "Oh, of course!" But it was such a cool solution for so many ways. For one, this fight ended up dovetailing into a later Cora scene that otherwise wouldn't have been possible and an ending we didn't even yet realize the book would desperately need. But also, it opened a tiny door in the narrative — a loophole that we'll surely exploit in later books and hint at in this first book's final scene. Because it implied that contrary to lore, the people of Waldron's Gate had found quiet ways to dream after all.

As to the yo-yo back and forth in the beats, that could be solved in the same fell swoop as addressing the tightening of the pace and arresting the word count sprawl. We didn't need to show all of Eila's actions every day; we could simply write a "time passes" chapter and allow weeks to fade with a few hundred words. The intention of those beats wasn't to give a diary account of Eila's days; we merely wanted to establish a slow decay in several pressures upon our heroine's shoulders.

We wanted the reader to see how hard it was becoming for Eila to keep feet in both worlds — in Pavilion, where she felt like a traitor to her city and her father, and in Waldron's Gate, where she toiled at the Ministry under the burden of terrible guilt.

We wanted to follow the progressive, bleeding change in Eila as she struggled to kick her Crumble addiction. She wouldn't be able to go cold turkey, we knew. She'd slip, like any addict. We didn't need a laundry list of when she slipped and when she climbed back on the wagon. We just needed to know it was happening.

We wanted to see the slow, dawning realization in Eila's mind as it became obvious that life was not going to resume as it had been, and that going forward was the only way out ... with Daw, with the Guile, and away from the Ministry.

Lastly, we wanted to paint Eila as a reverse junkie. Instead of lying and hiding her drug addiction from her parents, she'd need to lie and hide her *lack* of addiction. We wanted her to feel guilty. We wanted her to become increasingly sure that her insightful, already suspicious father knew she was up to something, and we wanted the notion to crawl under Eila's skin.

I left our Day Twenty meeting knowing full well what to do: I'd have the girls get into a fight over Levi, and then I'd write a "time passes" chapter where over the course of weeks, Eila struggles, lives a double life, and meets the Guile. It would be smooth sailing after that.

Wrong.

Day Twenty-One

There are many ways to write, and we're careful in our books and podcast to emphasize that we're in no way advocating our way as the standard to follow. Some people do best as pure "plotters," outlining events with the intricacy of a Swiss watchmaker. Others are pure "pantsers," flying by the seat of their pants at all times and eschewing advance structure beforehand. Most are probably somewhere between those two extremes. You should follow whatever works for you.

But one thing I love about the way Sean and I write together is that Sean's preproduction work gives me an almost checklist-like buffet of actions, events, and character quirks that I can use when I need them, with the timing sometimes entirely at my discretion. To recall a metaphor I used earlier, it's like having an extensive palate of paint colors and accompanying brushes of all sizes. Which I use when is up to me, and thankfully my partner has provided me with plenty of options.

I do think in terms of "Now this happens, and now this happens." But I also think in terms of "I can handle this here, and wouldn't this be cool to add here?"

The addition of that "time passes" chapter let me check off a lot of our story's backlogged to-do list in just a few hours.

Eila's guilt over lying? *Check.*

Eila's growing ambivalence about her job and suspicions of the Ministry? *Check.*

Eila meets the Guile — the revolutionary group Daw heads in Pavilion? *Check.*

Explaining the members of the Guile and their quirks to the readers? *Check.*

I spent one chapter checking all those boxes and many more, ticking through as much of what I still needed to say (but hadn't found a place to say yet) as possible, in one chapter that would catch the reader up. Sean's sprawling beats collapsed like a tent, many chapters becoming one and many trips up and down relaxing into mere mentions rather than diatribes, and we found ourselves neatly back on track. Action could resume. The climax could, finally, rise.

There's a maxim in writing that goes, "Show, don't tell." Like most maxims, we think it's bullshit. Yes, a good story-teller should use action and dialogue to explain what needs explaining most of the time rather than devolving into repeated info dumps from a narrator's point of view, but we don't agree that it's unacceptable to ever "tell." All stories have a rhythm, and that rhythm must accommodate the writer's needs (to pass certain information to the reader) as well as what the so-called experts claim is the "proper" way to write. *There is no one proper way to write.* Get that out of your head. Too many writers never begin because some snooty teacher once told them that a preposition is a bad thing to end a sentence with.

(See what I did there?)

Chapter 16 of *The Dream Engine* is very "tell-heavy." There is no dialogue, no "This is happening right now" action, and, at the end, a paragraph about each of the six remaining members of the Guile. The chapter is short (I handle such sections at a sprint, knowing most readers will only allow you so much time in "tell mode" before it begins to bleat in their ear), but it accomplished all of our aims, clearing the deck for what was to come.

I was sailing once past it. I wrote a scene that both illuminated a growing friendship between Savannah of the Guile and Eila and told the reader about the mysterious tunnels the Guile explored under Pavilion. I wrote another scene between Eila and Levi to follow, which gave the reader an idea of how near Eila was to her breaking point. So far, so good.

Then Eila went into training with Daw, using a Blunderbuss clone machine to enter a mental construct where, according to Sean's beats, she was supposed to separate real items from fantasy ones.

I hit a wall. And called our second emergency meeting in a row.

The problem, I told Sean, was that 1) I had no idea what Eila was supposed to be learning in her training and 2) the nature of the training was fundamentally flawed.

If Eila's goal was to learn something that would allow her to pierce the Fog for the members of the Guile to cross it, she'd need to do some kind of mind juju to make the fantasy beasts (remember how this all started as steampunk *Lord of the Rings*?) retreat, or defeat them, or something else. So how was telling fantasy from reality any good in terms of battle or defense? Once she was actually up *in* the Fog, how would work on a machine translate to facing real dragons and trolls in front of her? And most of all, how was this conception of real versus not real sensible in the least? Anything in the Fog would be *real* simply due to the fact that it existed in front of her, right? Even if it wasn't *supposed* to be real (and had been spun out of someone's dream and rejected by the Blunderbuss's Pavilion Dreamers as waste, like orcs or something), it still *would* be real if she ran into it, right?

Through the first half of the meeting, we spun laps around the ideas of real versus not, realizing that we must sound like two guys wearing berets and spouting philosophy in some hipster college coffeehouse. The semantics were thick and tangled. How could we possibly make rules about reality clashing with artifice, and how could Eila's training change those things enough to matter?

I certainly didn't know. Before calling Sean in, I'd tried to work it out with Daw Blackburn. I'd spent a half hour or so using Eila's words to ask Daw what the hell he was talking about. Often, when I don't understand parts of a story, this strategy will help me to riddle them out. The *Unicorn Western* saga is full of these moments: Clint (our grizzled gunslinger) asking Edward (his jerky unicorn partner) to explain the world to him. For the first time ever, though, I'd encountered a character less accommodating than Edward. Daw answered all of my questions with nonsensical riddles. He was, frankly, being an obtuse fucker.

In the end, we decided to lean into what we'd already established: Daw implying that sanity (and hence reality) were a matter of opinion. We didn't totally understand that idea ourselves, but the underpinnings were enough to give us a "hatch" that we could populate later. We only knew that the training had to progress, becoming harder and harder and less and less distinct, until Eila not only failed — but actually surrendered in screaming frustration. Because the lesson, we decided, was that real versus not real didn't actually matter. The lesson was coming to accept that often a person can't know what's real and what's right — and that learning to live with that unknowing edge of insanity was the only way she'd ever be able to survive with a cluttered, off-Crumble mind.

Or, as the singer Seal would say it, "We're never gonna survive ... unless we get a little crazy."

Day Twenty-Two

The longer I sit with an idea (and the more virtual paper I slay poring it over — throat-clearing words that Sean eventually edits out), the more it starts to make sense. And so, as I finished Eila's training scene, I was beginning to understand the lesson she hadn't yet grasped.

The human mind is a messy thing. Sometimes we see things wrong. Sometimes our memories change depending on what we want to or need to believe. Sometimes we think a person feels a certain way about us only to later learn that it was "all in our head," and sometimes we imagine ourselves as different than others perceive us.

Sometimes we're sure of things that turn out to be false.

Sometimes we disbelieve things with all our hearts, only to learn later that they're true after all.

A dominant theme throughout much Platt and Truant work is that there is no true good and no true bad, and that what we call evil is usually just the flip side of a coin. We continuously return to the idea that darkness is as important as light — an idea that, in my mind at least, always recalls the creatures from the children's movie *The Dark Crystal*, wherein a race of ancient beings was split into halves that were pure good and pure evil. You'd think the purely good Mystics would be aces, and that any sensible person could discard the evil Skeksis without a thought, but that's not the way it is. We need both halves of ourselves in order to be whole.

And so, unsurprisingly, here we were again in our YA debut, culling the notion that a whole person had to be at least a little damaged. Waldron's Gate was a fine place to live on first glance, but throughout the story the reader should begin to get a creeping suspicion that their existence is somewhat hollow. A thousand years of the Blunderbuss giving them what they need straight from the subconscious mind of its citizens rather than forcing them through the trial and error that comes with hands-on innovation had left their minds atrophied. Even those who worked the Blunderbuss didn't understand it; their cities were a cobbled-together mishmash because it was anyone's guess how a manifested-from-nothing waterwheel should work in harmony with a manifested-from-nothing clock tower. The people of Waldron's Gate didn't truly create. They didn't

dream. They didn't, in all likelihood, even really fantasize —
or possibly yearn and desire. What would love be like in a
world like that, where the prospect of not-having isn't there
to make someone grateful to have?

I pushed through the training scene and what followed
with that idea firmly in mind: that in order to experience
joy, we must have pain. To experience certainty, we must
have uncertainty. To dream true dreams, we must have
nightmares.

I found Daw, now strangely cooperative, saying the following — which, though we didn't know it yet, would set a
rich callback for the book's climactic moment:

> "Horrors. Dreams that cause you to wake in
> a sweat or with a scream. The mind's dirt work-
> ing upward, percolating out in order to cleanse
> you. Or perhaps to soil you, because sometimes
> our wounds make us who we are." Daw un-
> crossed his legs and leaned forward, now hands
> to knees, lightly clasped. He was near enough
> to touch her, but met Eila's eyes like a reluctant
> teacher. "Right now you are like a girl with her
> eyes closed who believes she can see the world
> with her hands. But if you don't open your eyes,
> you will never know the meaning of blue."

After the training, I again found myself deviating from
Sean's beats and following Eila as if she were a guide and I
were an unwitting tagalong. Sean had called for Eila to put
in a shift at the Ministry, realize she no longer fit, and head
home to dream a final, very important dream. But I wasn't
buying it. Eila had been beaten up pretty badly by now, and
given her temperament I figured she'd have grown a strange

shell of mixed apathy and furious strength. She'd reached the stage where nothing seemed to matter and nothing ever went right, where she failed with Daw even while trying to do the thing she didn't want to do. That made her a loose-cannon sort of dangerous, because she had very little left to lose.

I didn't want her to simply leave. I wanted Eila to have a showdown. So I sent her to see her supervisor at the Ministry of Manifestation, Rabbit Brampton.

I don't want to lose any of the less scholarly among you by delving into jargon, but Rabbit Brampton is what is known in literary circles as "a giant dickhead." He's a snippy little Caesar who rules Eila's section of the Ministry like his own condescending kingdom, and thus far Eila had taken his abuse because she was fifteen and in his employ. But when Brampton calls her into his office to discuss her underperformance on the great engine, Eila finds herself growing a pair.

She suddenly suspects that if anyone knows about the machine's torturous true nature, Brampton must. They verbally tussle, Brampton getting angrier and angrier until Eila lets slip that she's been working on the Blunderbuss while off Crumble.

At this point, I got the feeling that Brampton would freak out, and he did. He ran out, locking Eila in his office, flustered and bustling. But Eila, coming into her power, can both Dream and Build. And so just as she did when she created a door on the Convenience machine leading down into Pavilion, she manifests an open lock and calmly leaves the building.

I loved the scene, but I didn't know what it meant and still don't. What *does* happen when a Builder works the Blunderbuss off Crumble? Clearly it's bad, but neither of us knows that particular truth even now. It's a hatch. We'll figure it out later.

All that mattered was that the scene ended in a way that meant Eila couldn't go home.

I knew from Sean's beats that the essential next step was for Eila to go to sleep, because she needed to have a disastrous dream that would finally roil the story's rising action to a boil.

Eila couldn't sleep in her bed. She'd burned her final bridge, and it seemed that authorities might pursue her.

It seemed to me that the authorities might watch the trolleys too, which meant she couldn't head to the Doer district, to the Convenience staircase, and sneak down to Pavilion.

It took me a while to puzzle out where Eila might lay her head that night, but when I did, something inside me sighed, because as always happens when we have faith in our story, the little loose ends were all coming together.

Of course. She'd contact Cora.

Day Twenty-Three

I apologized halfheartedly to Sean when I scheduled our Day Twenty-Three story meeting. I said that I'd hoped to plow through the end of the book without requiring another discussion, but that there were too many loose ends and I had be sure they all fit just right. But we could be quick, because I knew the broad strokes and had just one day left in the draft. The meeting was simply a matter of hashing out a few final details.

In retrospect, this was hilarious. In truth, we had at least three full days' worth of writing (jammed into two days) and a three-hour, the sky-is-falling story meeting still to come. But that particularly sticky revelation was, at the time, still in the future.

I'd spent the morning painting a quiet, twilit scene between Eila and Cora, in a childhood treehouse the friends had shared at an orchard in the country. The scene is sweet and subtle, meant to contrast the prior scene with Brampton and remind the reader that Eila, though she's grown stronger, is still vulnerable. The scene brought back all that we'd learned about Cora and Eila. Cora is kind; Eila is selfish. But Cora is forgiving, and though she was angry and hurt, she'd never turn from her friend in her time of need. This was also all necessary stuff for the book's final scene, though we were still a ways from that discovery.

They fall asleep. Eila dreams again of her nightmarescape in the middle of a storybook arena called the Citadel, this time home to a vision of Rabbit Brampton who argues (quite convincingly) that Eila, who's so sure she's right in all of this desperate madness, might turn out to be the crazy one. I wanted to twist the knife deeper in Eila's wound, deepening her own doubts about whether her actions are the correct ones ... or whether, by contrast, her way of seeing the world might not be accurate after all.

You dream of rebellions, like any desperate child, Dream-Brampton berates her. *You dream of a handsome suitor come to save you from mediocrity. And yet the world is wrong, and you are right? You stand in the middle of a stone arena that doesn't exist ... and believe that you must be correct, while everyone else is wrong?*

A dragon enters the scene, forcing Eila to flee. But when she awakes, Eila realizes that Cora is shaking her with the news that the world has gone topsy-turvy because — as impossible as it seems — a dragon has been shot down outside the city.

As our "final" story meeting began we had a reasonably clear idea of what had to happen next. Eila had accidentally pulled a dragon from her dream the way she'd pulled an artifact from a prior dream, but this time her loss of control had shoved the situation past its breaking point. Nobody knew what was in the Fog, or that the fantasy creatures from their fables were real — that they'd been plucked from Alterra's subconscious and shuttled outside as mental waste. Alterra was in a state of panic, and Daw and the Guile could no longer bide their time. It would force Eila to act *now*, whether she felt prepared or not, and urge our book toward its conclusion.

The ending, as we envisioned it, was simple. She'd run to Pavilion, watch the Guile head up the tunnels and toward the Fog, then operate the Blunderbuss clone machine to help them on their quest. We had the perfect ending scene in mind: They'd emerge on the other side of the Fog to find themselves on a beach, and an enormous, city-sized space ship would be floating there waiting. That ending would do several things. One, it would make the reader want to continue the series to find out what the hell the giant ship was all about. Two, it would open up an enormous world outside of Alterra for us to play in with subsequent books. And three, it would open the world for the people watching us write the book. We'd already framed the world of Alterra as open-source fiction, meaning that we were encouraging those writers to create their own books in our world, to publish them, and to keep all the profits for themselves. The ship was a hatch, yes. And no, we didn't have any idea what it meant or where it had come from. But it was good enough to pry open the door — to peek beyond the Fog enough to let everyone play.

Yet, that ending felt anticlimactic. Eila wouldn't even be *in* the Fog; she'd be working the machine in Pavilion while *the Guile* went through the Fog. And even then, Eila wasn't facing anything more interesting than assorted horrors. Yes, the Fog was terrifying, but we hadn't given Eila a "big boss" to fight in her final scene. So what if she fought goblins and demons? How was that any different from any action scene, and how was it worthy of the novel's climax?

We set out to do two things through the course of our discussion. First, we wanted Eila to enter the Fog herself rather than simply piloting the way for others. And second, we needed to give her something bigger to face — something we'd built up to for the entire novel.

But of course, we hadn't built up to anything yet, so we added it to our list of things we had to "reverse foreshadow" during the polish, along with the idea that Cora always carried a beloved sketchpad. All we needed now were a boogeyman and a way to force Eila to stare it down.

Getting Eila off the machine seemed easy. We could have something go wrong with the thing, necessitating a sprint up the tunnels to go help in a more direct way. This would lead to a "Dumbo's feather" moment, wherein Eila realizes she doesn't need the machine at all, that she can Dream and Build just fine without it. We had a vague idea that she'd somehow save the day, leaving me to work out the cinematic details.

Finding a boogeyman was harder, but we quickly settled on fire. Eila would be afraid of fire — but not just in a vague way; it had to be mortal, personal, vulnerably terrifying to her core. The seeds were planted: Dragons breathed fire, so the Fog's haunted forest itself might be aflame. To counterbalance the present day, we gave Eila a scarring childhood memory: that of a friendly baker who owned a shop she and Juliette used to visit before he was trapped inside during a fire and burned alive.

But that wasn't quite enough. We had all the pieces (Eila to Pavilion, Guile into the Fog, Eila into the Fog while battling fire, triumph and getting through the Fog to find the waiting ship), but it still felt flat. Because really, why had so much of the book occurred if readers would simply watch our heroine overcome a rather mundane fear and battle fantasy creatures with her mind? What of her training sessions? What of the Dream Engine itself? What of our themes: Uncertainty is inevitable and reality and sanity were a matter of opinion? If she simply battled through, it was all a waste of time. Literary masturbation, navel gazing for the sake of gazing at a navel.

All great protagonists change through the course of a story, and that usually means a revelation. We needed to know that in the end, because of *all* she'd been through and *all* she's learned (not just in the climax), Eila was forever different, and her world would never be the same.

Did overcoming a fear of fire do that? Nope, not in the least.

We asked ourselves how Eila could learn a lesson. We were pretty sure what that lesson was, because Sean and Daw Blackburn had both said it: She had to realize that a healthy person's mind was inherently flawed, and that a sane mind had plenty of capacity for insanity. These were ideas unknown in Waldron's Gate. And why? Because of what Daw had said about the nature of nightmares:

The mind's dirt working upward, percolating out in order to cleanse you. Or perhaps to soil you, because sometimes our wounds make us who we are.

Eila was no longer a lithium Barbie, safely pacified by Crumble. Unlike the rest of her fellows topside, she was damaged and wounded. And so somehow we needed her to see that imperfections made her strong and able to do what nobody else could.

Listening back to that meeting recently, I realized that although we were enthusiastic about Eila learning this lesson and agreed it would make the book sizzle, we never actually got to the point where we decided how she'd learn it.

But that was okay, because I didn't make it that far before realizing quite obviously that the entire ending, as conceived, was dead wrong.

Day Twenty-Four

There was plenty to celebrate when we met, yet again, on Day Twenty-Four. Sean was evolving the world documents that other authors would use to write in our open-source fiction world — an industry first at its scope, allowing others to publish in our world without paying us royalties. We had a nearly complete version of the book's gorgeous cover, which our illustrator Erin had nailed. We were only six days from the end of the project, and the Unboxers were such that I allowed myself to peek past the blinders and see them, standing and cheering for us as we neared the finish line.

The only problem was that even after my "final" day writing, the draft wasn't done. Before we could give our watchers the finished book, we had to publish it. Before we could publish it, I needed to run through it a final time. Before I could run through it, our editor had to see it... and before that, Sean had to finish *his* polish. That was stalled until Sean completed his first pass, which he simply terms an edit. And it was tricky to see how Sean could edit the draft until I fished it, which I had no idea how to do because it was all wrong.

I texted Sean:

> *Something just occurred to me. Do you think Eila battling through the Fog to find a cliffhanger waiting is a strong enough "closing" for this book, considering it's a novel and not a serial?*

I remember my heart pounding when I sent that text. I almost hadn't wanted to send it, because if I turned my head and ignored the suspicion I'd had in my gut, maybe it would go away. I was poking at something I didn't want to poke by voicing my concern instead of wrestling past it. I sent it in the spirit of a wife asking her husband if she looks fat. I didn't really want to know the truth. I needed my partner to say what I wanted to hear.

Sean's reply came back, somehow more deadpan than a text message has any right to sound. I could almost hear the somber tone in his voice through those little digital letters on my iPhone:

> *No. It's not. We need to figure that out.*

Sean and Dave have a full year on me as professional writers, and they spent that year doing big things. My favorite is crowning themselves "Kings of the Serial," because although they don't remotely pretend to have invented serialization, they were arguably the first to wrap both hands around it as a concept translatable to ebooks. Sean and

Dave are used to writing serialized episodes, then wrapping six episodes into a season. Never ones to fix what isn't broken, Sean and I adopted the same model at Realm & Sands, writing several serials ourselves.

A written serial, like a television serial, barely needs to close a story arc within a single episode. It can and should end on a cliffhanger that (delightfully) frustrates the reader as much as it pleases her. Seasons need to close a few story arcs, but tend to open even more. Season cliffhangers in serials are like written jerks, leaving the best fans screaming at the authors for leaving them hanging.

In *The Dream Engine*, we had rising action. We had some barely-closed story lines, such as the key one about whether or not the Guile would make it through the Fog. We had a big cliffhanger with the ship at sea, and we'd both imagined our novel fading to black right there, leaving mouths agape.

But we hadn't answered so many questions. We hadn't closed most of the boxes. What happened with Cora? What happened with Eila's parents, and her father's suspicions? What happened at the Ministry? What of Eila's Crumble dependency, and the niggling feeling that she should maybe tell a few others of its ravages?

They were all good questions for a serial, but that's not what we'd written. We'd spent June on a *book*. And yes, it was the first book in a series, so the story *would* continue and we *did* want readers curious to know what would happen next. But in a book — even a series book — the rules are different. Before you can open a new wound to make readers curious, you must close the old one. Serials can roll along at sixty miles per hour and then stop dead, pounding the cliffhanger like an actual cliff. Series novels don't have the right. They need to end most of the way, leaving pinholes for questions rather than giant gaping chasms.

We'd imagined Eila's flight through the Fog as something frantic. They'd get out, but barely. Because how could you defeat the Fog? And they'd find themselves out but still trapped, still wondering, with that big ship there making everyone gasp. And then... *DUN DUN DUNNN!...* we'd pick up where we'd left off in Book 1, missing only the taunting "To be continued ... "

But if we did that, we'd be breaking a covenant with the reader. They would be pissed. No one wants to finish a one hundred thousand-word novel with blue balls. We'd be eviscerated, and deserve it.

How had this happened? We both knew better. We needed Eila to defeat something, but we'd given her nothing to defeat. Getting past fire isn't the same as defeating the flames. Getting through the Fog isn't achieving victory over the horror. It didn't matter what revelation she'd had or what lesson she'd learned. Her story would dangle just the same.

I typed back:

Shit.

It was Day Twenty-Four. We had miles of postproduction before us and no finished product to produce. We hadn't built up to anything, so had nothing to conclude. There was no enemy. There was no oppressor other than the state itself, and most everyone seemed oblivious to society's foundations anyway. Waldron's Gate was milquetoast, with little obvious strife. Pavilion was technically oppressed, but had no idea. Only Daw and the Guile knew the score as far as we were aware, plus possibly someone like Rabbit Brampton. It would be a war of a dozen, with no army behind them.

The first hour of that marathon meeting was murder. We spun in circles, recalling the stomach-sinking feeling of the disastrous first Day Three meeting, before we rose like phoenixes that afternoon. The difference now was that we didn't have twenty-seven days. We had six. And we couldn't spark a story idea out of nothing as we had that day, because our story was already written.

We asked, "Who's the enemy? Whom can she defeat?"

Again, answers were elusive. We toyed with the idea of having the Waldron's Gate government be the enemy, but aside from any sort of overthrow feeling impossibly rushed (nine-five thousand words of quiet, philosophical action and dream sequences plus five thousand words of sudden rebellion? The Guile might as well declare, "Nobody expects the Spanish Inquisition!" while they were at it; it was a pretty toothless enemy. We'd hinted at a prime minister, but he'd never even been seen. There were no *1984* dark agencies in play with sinister agendas; there was only the Ministry of Manifestation where even the people at the top seemed to be following orders. We'd opted for a sighing sort of oppression, where nobody rose up because nobody really thought anything was wrong. Even Pavilion's Dreamers did their nasty jobs voluntarily, with a sense of grim duty.

What about a broadcast? Could the Guile send out a pirate signal with a message? Maybe, but what would they say? Were they supposed to give an answer to a question no Alterran was asking? Offer a solution to a problem nobody seemed to feel they had? And even that left the sticky matter of making it happen. Even if we'd had weeks to craft final scenes, it would feel like one of those movies that never quite ends, where the action just kind of goes on and on, fatiguing the viewer. And besides, Eila would be in the Fog, battling demons. Was she supposed to then rush *back* through the Fog from the far side, head to a broadcast tower in the city, and grab a steampunk microphone like Happy Harry Hard-On in *Pump Up the Volume*?

We puzzled. And puzzled. And puzzled.

Finally Sean got the idea to make Crumble the enemy. It made sense. The country was addicted, but nobody thought there was anything wrong. If she could wake the nation ... just wake them up! ... that might be enough.

Or would it? There was still no battle. You couldn't battle Crumble, other than in the way that Eila already had. And we still didn't know how she could tell anyone without a broadcast.

We returned to Eila's lessons — what Daw had been trying to show her on the Blunderbuss clone in Pavilion. And after some mulling, we found the first seeds of our solution.

It had to do with Atwell, Eila's father.

She couldn't battle Crumble, true. But Eila *could* battle something unreal that represented Crumble's influence, feeling that thing as real, feeling it begin to prickle her skin with doubt about everything she'd done. Eila's training had already pointed toward a solution: During her first days off the drug, Daw's training showed her two things, side-by-side. One was her father, clean shaven. The other was her father, his face speckled with stubble — a habit Atwell Doyle had whenever he was puzzling a problem. Eila had asked Daw which problem the stubbled Atwell was trying to solve, and Daw had told her: *whether or not his daughter is a traitor.*

Unknowingly, we'd already made the leap necessary for our battle with Crumble. Crumble lets the Blunderbuss steal a person's dreams, but in the process it numbs them, thieving away all the internal mental "dirt" that Daw had insisted needed to "work upward in order to cleanse you." This was our trope yet again, of both darkness and light being necessary. Without Crumble, Eila's mind became flawed and uncertain — a state that you and I (and Pavilion dwellers) accept as normal, but that frightened Eila at first. She became unsure of things she'd previously never questioned, such as whether or not a coat hook on the wall looked like a sinister hand ... or whether or not her actions, though nobly intended, made her a traitor to her father.

I think if we'd started out with the thematic thought, "Let's use this book to question the nature of reality, belief, and the Jungian 'shadow,'" we'd have come off as pretentious assholes. But the idea had surfaced nonetheless [Eila faced not only obvious real/not-real pairings like fairies versus people, but also differing instances of her mother (one of whom loved her and one of whom didn't), herself (one of whom was crazy and one of whom was sane)], and so we knew we had to use it. What felt like mental dirt and corruption and damage to Eila was simply the true nature of her mind. She was flawed, and the Fog would attempt to exploit those flaws, to try and urge Eila back onto Crumble. She'd mostly kicked her addiction, but now she'd face it again, as she stared into the specter of her betrayed father in the Fog.

We knew, of course, that the Atwell Doyle Eila encounters after running through the tunnels to enter the Fog would be a fiend to test her and force her back into addiction, but we had to make the reader believe he was real. That necessitated foreshadowing that wasn't in place.

But as one hour's worth of meeting dragged into two then three, we saw light teasing the tunnel's end. I was planning to go over the whole manuscript again anyway, and would simply have to add that foreshadowing as I went.

We needed a reason for Eila to believe that her father was in the Fog, so we had her see a man at the border once she was inside, thinking him a reporter there to cover the dragon's sudden appearance. But he'd set down a battered leather briefcase, which Eila would later realize, panicking in the faux Blunderbuss down in Pavilion, was her father's ... a briefcase I'd have to allude to a time or two in the past as an Atwell-specific signature.

We needed the reader to believe that the *real* Atwell (not a spook conjured by the Fog) would actually enter the Fog. Fortunately, we'd already seen that Atwell doubted his daughter's tales and thought her either unstable or up to something. I merely needed to reinforce all of that and add some more attributes to Atwell's character, then have Eila reason out Atwell's most likely thought process later: He wasn't the kind of man who stood back and waited for something inevitable to happen. Eila had always feared the Fog, and he'd taught his daughter to face her fears. He was a logical man. We believed he'd rightly conclude that Eila was in the Fog, then enter to save her.

And perhaps most importantly, we needed a way for Eila, at her moment of revelation, to know the false Atwell for the bogey he was. We decided that the best way to handle that was to have the false Atwell say something in the Fog that Eila feared him saying ... but that, at the critical moment, she'd realize wasn't actually true.

Which is real? Daw had repeatedly asked her. And we'd need Eila, as Atwell said what he needed to say, to understand her father's love *was real*. His belief in her. Not her petty, insecure fears. She'd have to understand, too, that she'd never truly *know* anything and that there would always be shades of gray. You couldn't survive in the real world if you always needed to be sure. You had to know that things might be wrong, and that the horrors you suspected may or may not exist. And that in the end it didn't matter because you had to go on living anyway.

At that critical juncture, we decided that the fake Atwell would express extreme disappointment in Eila's decision to join Aether Forefront (the Ministry's creative wing) instead of Enigma (its analytical, engineering wing). We had no concept of either wing in place, so I added seeding their mentions to my list, along with a scene in which Atwell earnestly tells his daughter, "I am proud of you, no matter what you choose."

BOOM. Lesson learned.

BOOM. Big bad guy defeated.

There was still the matter of Eila informing the populace about Crumble as a means to drag pacified Alterrans into the next book, but we worked that bit out in the final hour, as the last of our energy was draining away.

I proposed the solution, but it took a while for Sean to warm up to it: What if instead of telling the final chapter (after Eila and the Guile discover the spaceship over the water) from Eila's point of view, we tell it from Cora's? It would take place a few weeks after Eila mysteriously vanished, after the Alterran government has explained away the dragon as a secret military project. Cora's doubts about what Eila had told her — about Pavilion, the Blunderbuss, and the Fog — would have had time to steep, arousing curiosity. Curiosity would beget emotion. And emotion, through the loophole we left around Eila's ability to sketch Levi in the past, would beget a strange and guarded kind of dreaming.

Cora is feeling her melancholy, beginning to question what she'd once taken for granted. Starting to feel loose ends within her mind, as if her sanity is unraveling. In that state, she has her broadcast unit (TV) on and sees a strange pirate transmission featuring Eila with a background the reader will understand must be aboard the strange ship.

Eila issues a challenge to Alterran citizens who, in the past weeks of hushed-up turmoil, have begun to feel the edge of something rising in their minds. She tells them to go off Crumble, and "let the wild things inside."

The transmission terminates. The final scene is Cora flushing her Crumble down the toilet, whispering a line that Eila had told her earlier (that we'd go back and *have* Eila tell her earlier), in the treehouse: "Crazy is what happens when you start to believe."

BOOM. Message delivered, and the sequel's box of curiosities successfully opened.

I had a lot of writing left, but didn't care. We were in the homestretch. I could finish the climax and resolution in a day, then handle the foreshadowing to that climax during the polish.

We were finally nearing the finish line. The tunnel's light grew brighter.

We'd had our own Crumble-like doubts, staring down two versions of *The Dream Engine* while Daw Blackburn growled in our ears: *One of them is a failure, and the other is a success.*

Day Twenty-Four began under the gun with no solution in sight, a roadkill of words before us. We simply didn't know.

Which is real? Daw seemed to say.

Three characters had epiphanies that day, and only one was fictional.

Which is real – the triumph or the flop?

But we'd held fast to our faith. We'd kept working, hammering on the nut, and sawing at the knots, believing no problem lives without its solution. Our faith paid us back with an answer we loved.

The clock stood at six days to midnight.

We were going to make it.

APPLY IT! This Chapter's Takeaways and Action Steps

Here's the least you need to know from this chapter:

- Know your story's goals in order to know your ending. In our case, we should have remembered we were trying to write a series book ... *not a serial.* That's why we had to scramble so much at the end.

- Don't be afraid to trash what you have in the service of something better. We learned that many times along the way and toward the end, too.

- "Show, don't tell," like most maxims, is only a rough rule of thumb.

- If you feel uncertain, keep talking and brainstorming until you find the solution. There is *always* a solution if you're creative enough to insist on its discovery.

- Most of all and at all times, *have faith in your story.*

And here are two things you can do RIGHT NOW to apply this chapter's lessons:

- Take your beats from the earlier assignment and completely alter your ending. Remember, not even good ideas are sacred. Because there are no truly good ideas. There are only good writers willing to make any idea good or great.

- Write yourself into an impossible corner, leaving yourself unsure how to resolve a problem. Then return the next day and figure out a way to solve it.

CHAPTER NINE:
Wrapping Up (And Beginning Again)

I RECEIVED A SMALL PACKAGE in the mail today. It held my business cards, which Sean, Dave, and I just had printed. Sean and I needed them because we're going to be delivering the closing keynote at a conference in a few weeks. Dave will probably bury his in the back yard. I strongly suspect he'll have decoy cards printed with a fake name and a phony e-mail address so that nobody can ever find him in his lair of paranoia.

The three of us sweated for a while over the job titles on those cards, all of which list our business as the parent company of Sterling & Stone, not the specific imprints that we most commonly call home. At Realm & Sands, I'm lead writer, whereas Sean is the story architect — but at Sterling & Stone, which also encapsulates Sean and Dave's Collective Inkwell imprint? That's harder.

We wouldn't admit it, but we all wanted titles that made us sound important. Sean, who created Sterling & Stone before making us all equal partners, suggested he be Founder — or (and to his credit, he knew this was pretentious) Visionary. Dave made the most sense as Creative Director, though it wasn't quite on the mark, and I was pitched as something like Word Machine, which was terrible but the closest we could figure.

Today, as I looked at my new card, I read the job title that all three of us ended up deciding to share: *STORYTELLER.* Something shifted inside, because seeing that word, there below my name, made it real in a way that nothing had before. I would hand that card to people who asked what I did, and the card would declare the truth in a way that only 16-point card stock can: *I tell stories for a living.*

I've told stories all my life, so it's strange to think that a card gave me permission to believe it. I think that's the way it is for many writers, and specifically the target audience for *Fiction Unboxed.* We said as much in our Kickstarter video, which felt a thousand years old on the day I was finishing *The Dream Engine's* draft: "For many writers, that sense of possibility comes crashing down when they try to share the stories inside them because they've been sold on a lie. They've been taught to believe that telling stories is hard. But is it?"

In the context of that video, the question is rhetorical and meant to be answered with a "No," but I could easily see people challenging us. *Of course it's not easy to tell stories, or everyone would be a writer. Everyone would be a great writer.* But that wasn't what we were saying at all. We didn't say that being a writer, a great writer, a competent writer, or a best-selling writer were easy; we said that *telling stories* is easy. And of course it is. Humanity has been telling tales since the dawn of language, back when "Mammoth chase Gork" was a scintillating cliffhanger. Ever since guys started saying, "A man walks into a bar," and we waited to find out what would happen next.

On the morning of Day Twenty-Five — even though I didn't have my official business card yet — I knew we'd delivered on our promise to demystify the art of telling stories. Anyone could tell them, and a writer's job was to do the work and practice required to write them well. We'd taken nothing and spun it into a rather complex story — and we'd done it blind, stumbling forward with only the vaguest notion of where we were headed. Going forward so haphazardly had been foolhardy and dangerous. Anything could have happened.

What if we weren't given an amazing idea? (We weren't; we spun our wheels for three days before Sean wrote a single sentence during a brief respite that formed our book's entire underpinnings.)

What if we wrote ourselves into a corner? (We did, and we wiggled right out of it.)

What if we got blocked about what should happen next? (We did, often, and talked until the block dissolved.)

Or — God forbid! — what if we screwed up the ending? (We did that too.)

The solution was always to keep moving forward. Keep talking. Keep figuring. Keep writing, and always trust the story to unfold as it's supposed to.

Our stories, friends, create themselves.

If you can accept that we are merely scribes sent to record what happens in those stories, one type of magic vanishes while another type of magic — more abundant, more special, and far more accessible — will, with practice and hard work, start to sift through your fingertips.

I could feel that magic on that final day of writing. And I could feel it as I smoothed our story's furrows, polishing it again from the beginning, bringing the still-hidden gems to the surface.

Day Twenty-Five

I may sound Pollyanna and kumbaya as I look back on the end of Day Twenty-Four as the moment we both knew how well *The Dream Engine* would turn out, but at the time it wasn't lost on me that we had less than a week left to pull off some rather large feats.

Slashing the Gordian knot to figure a proper ending was a significant accomplishment, but it was nowhere near the finish line. I still had to *write* that much more complex version of the ending, which meant putting down over twelve thousand words in a day. Sean then needed to finish his edit and polish, and the book's final sections had to pass through our editor's hands. After that, Sean had to comb through Jason's suggested edits and green-light those he agreed with. And only *then* could I read the entire 350-page manuscript again, making anal changes to every page in grammar and voice as I went, seeding mentions of key events and items that needed to appear later, rewriting parts of plot lines, and doing a ton of foreshadowing.

No big deal, right?

But on my last day of new creation, I couldn't worry about any of that. Sean had his hands full with *Fiction Unboxed* loose ends (the poor bastard ended up handling customer service all by himself because we didn't yet have any administrative help), and it was my job, come hell or high water, to *finish the draft*. I got up a few hours ahead of schedule, in the no man's land between what eager risers call early and revelers call late, and began pouring my time into words.

During that final session, my fingers screamed across the keys. Even allowing for coffee and bathroom breaks, I averaged over two thousand words per hour and held that pace for six hours straight.

I began in the wee hours with Eila still in Pavilion, safely away from the Fog's horrors, clearing a path for Levi and Walker with the use of her mind and the tinkered Blunderbuss clone machine. I knew now that Atwell had to seem as if he'd entered the Fog to find her, but that Eila must realize the truth only after it was too late. She had to see a man near the Fog's edge with a battered leather briefcase (the briefcase I'd add during the polish; the same briefcase that, although meaningful to us after the final story meeting, meant nothing at all to the people who'd been reading the story live). She had to continue helping the two men, who in turn had to battle some horrors of their own, then have her realization.

At that point Eila had to bolt out of the machine, leaving Phoebe to hold the opening (and fill it with fresh nightmares) as she ran up the tunnels and into the Fog for real.

I figured more tension was better, so I doubled down on our ideas from earlier and had her encounter the baker, Carlo, in an undead and highly crispy state — something Eila realizes was one of her own nightmares stolen long ago, then materialized as real in the Fog. This had a way of stacking more and more chips against Eila before she reached the climactic scene, forcing her to face fears that a dreaming mind would have faced as they happened, while they were simply nighttime visions. Carlos's appearance, in his burning bakery, also served the purpose of "breaking" Eila. By this scene's end, Eila finally reaches her limit in a way that 1) makes her father's appearance a great and terrible comfort (terrible because of how the scene unfolds), and 2) makes her mind (now even more "damaged") able to accept the strange truth of the scene still to come. In other words, the terrifying encounter with Carlo makes Eila feel as if her sanity may have snapped. But really, what has snapped is Eila's conviction that she must always feel safe and secure and certain.

I decided the scene with Eila and Atwell should be quiet. As it begins, Eila believes she's found her father — but thanks to what she's just been through, the actual feeling is more like him saving her than the other way around. Atwell isn't in trouble, nor is he angry. He saw how far her reality just bent, she feels, and knows how brittle her mind is. The scene's protective nature hopefully makes Atwell's concern convincing for Eila and the reader. All he wants is for his daughter to come out safely and get her broken mind back to normal. By going back on Crumble, where she belongs.

The scene itself wasn't hard to write; it's in these softer scenes (and, ironically, during violent arguments) when I'm most able to hear characters' true voices. I simply listened to their discussion, knowing how it had to proceed. Eila comes around when Atwell expresses his disappointment, recalling their earlier discussion (that I hadn't yet added to the draft). She remembers what he said about always being proud (which I hadn't added yet either), and how he'd never resent her decision to join Aether Forefront instead of the Enigma department (two things that were also waiting to exist).

Eila has her revelation. She dismisses the phantom, then realizes her power — to, within the Fog's rich creative soil, both Dream and Build without the aid of any machine — and cuts a path for herself, Levi, and Walker to follow.

Then I had to write the beach scene, where they discover the ship, ending on a cliffhanger, now that she'd properly defeated her own "big enemy" — Crumble addiction itself, and her mind refused to dip its toes into madness.

And finally, I had to finish the book from Cora's POV. Adding this final scene did two important things. One, it established the next book's stakes in a way that the ship over the ocean couldn't. Yes, the arrival of a massive ship meant plenty for Alterra, but it was a cold sort of meaning: here lies menace; here lies new frontiers. It didn't touch a reader's heart. But Cora? Cora had changed almost as much as Eila. Having sweet, innocent Cora — a sensible stand-in for the vulnerable soul of the entire population — decide to turn her back on the status quo and delve into disobedience made it all very personal. In that way, it enhances the cliffhanger. But conversely, adding the Cora scene allowed us to answer some questions we'd otherwise have left dangling — even if those answers amounted to little more than letting the reader know we hadn't forgotten the open boxes back home, like Atwell's position with the Ministry after his daughter went rogue and whether there was still widespread panic over the downed dragon.

We both love the way our book ended. It was strange to think that twenty-five days earlier, not a single thought about this new world had existed. And it was strange to recall that less than twenty-four *hours* earlier, almost none of the ending, as it turned out, had been conceived.

I sat back in my chair. I looked at the screen with a feeling of exhausted satisfaction, then closed my Scrivener window, sent Sean a text to let him know I was done, and packed up for the gym. I didn't celebrate, or jump up and down. I never do. In a way, it seems like the completion of a story should be something to celebrate, but I never have. Because not once, in thirty to fifty published works of fiction, depending on how you count, has the ending of a story felt like I've really *created* anything. In those moments, celebration wouldn't feel right or wrong; it would simply feel out of place. Because, what did *we* do? Sean and I were the scribes. We were the excavators. Eila and the others had done all the work.

I'd just spent twenty days staring at my monitor, watching an engrossing story unfold. But now the final curtain had fallen, and I as that story's faithful observer and recorder was free to leave the theater.

As always, the story had told itself.

Days Twenty-Six through Twenty-Nine

Look: We're not assholes. We get that writers write, that it's the creative juices that stir in an author's mind that allow stories to grow and prosper, yada yada yada. Are we proud of *The Dream Engine* in the way we'd be proud of something we actually created? Of course. Do we run around telling people, "Look at this cool story I found but did nothing to shape!" No, of course not.

When we say things like "Stories make themselves" and "We listen to what characters say and record it," part of that is the eye-rolling bullshit we authors (yes, you too) are permitted to spew because we're artists. But we do believe it, and the ability to both write a novel and excavate a story at the same time is our version of Eila realizing that maintaining her sanity means coming to grips with her own native *in*sanity.

Because plenty of writers in the real world take Crumble, too, you know. It doesn't come in capsules or a dusty block our handmaid sifts into her cooking, but it does come in the form of proscriptive language teachers, critical parents, personal fears about violating societal rules, and literary snobbery. If you listen to any of those things, that's Crumble's deception whispering in your ear. That's your own false Atwell Doyle, swearing that you've lost your mind if you think you can write and that you'd better flee the Fog — running to a safer and less embarrassing hobby collecting stamps or building model cars, perhaps — and return to your daily infusions of self-limiting bullshit.

Do you know why we're sure you can tell a story? Because stories are part of our culture. They're out there in humanity's fertile soil, awaiting excavation. To call all the way back to Sean's initially aborted ideas, you might say they're out there in the Akashic records. You don't need to be struck by a lightning bolt before you can sit to pen your tale. You need to stop dosing yourself with self-doubting Crumble, accept that any of us could pick up an idea, dust it off, and summon the stones to get started. Will you write a masterpiece? Maybe not. Will you write a decent book that doesn't make your friends want to cringe? Again, maybe not. But you can tell a story. Remember that. In some form, in some way, with some degree of facility, *you can tell a story*. And once you believe that, all you need is to practice, learn to listen to the tale's whisper, and practice some more.

A lot happened in the days that followed, as *Fiction Unboxed* wound down to a close. I didn't get any time off simply because the first draft was finished; I turned to my final polish bright and early the following morning. Sean was working double time on his end, editing and polishing, incorporating our editor's changes, shucking new pages off, and shining the Alterra world documents for Unboxers who wanted to tell their own tales.

We'd had a more-finished version of the cover back from Erin. The colors were a bit washed out because she had yet to add a final layer, but we didn't understand that and asked her for an enhanced version with some brass and copper accents added to make the Blunderbuss, behind Eila, pop. I'd finally come out of my isolation booth and got to listen as Unboxers weighed in on the cover ... and then as it all became moot with the reveal of Erin's final version of the original, which truly sang.

We were so happy on Day Twenty-Seven to hold the final Q&A for the live audience. It was the first time we could meet them with full confidence in our swollen hearts, able to look them in the eyes (virtually, of course) and proclaim that we'd done it. Until this point, the project had been fueled by our faith. I'm happy to say that our tribe's belief in our ability to see the story through to a satisfying end never wavered, and now they were jubilant. We accepted live questions as always, but it was hard to find the real questions that day because the comments were jammed with congratulations. As tired as Sean and I were, we were over the moon that day, grinning even wider than usual. I could finally answer questions about the story itself, now that my blinders were off. I *wanted* to discuss the story, because I knew it was good. We understood that not all Unboxers would be into a steampunk YA novel (or even a Platt and Truant book; we tend to be wordy and have a rather distinctive voice) because they were writers more than readers, but we were certain that Realm & Sands readers — our Truest Fans — would love it.

The project's pieces were settling into place. Sean had decided to read the story aloud through his polish, so the *Unboxed* updates turned to raw audio reads as they turned away from new draft words. He'd also recorded a series of live-edit videos in which he took screencast recordings as he plowed through, explaining what he changed from my original copy. Soon, we even had the first chapters of the professional audiobook back from our narrator, Ray Chase. Ray's read made the book come alive in a way that literally made me tear up during my quality-checking listen.

Sean dotted i's and crossed t's. He gave the chapters their final names (something that, like naming characters, he's a thousand times better at than I am) and wrote the front and back matter for the book, adding a dedication and the "thank you" list of our Kickstarter supporters as promised. He wrangled final cover arrangements with Erin, got our buddy Garrett started on the paperback and hardback versions of the book, and paced Ray's progress on the audiobook. He edited, polished, shuffled pages to Jason and back from Jason, from Jason to me.

Jason Whited, our editor on *The Dream Engine*, had embraced the crazy, breakneck speed of *Fiction Unboxed* as fully as Erin (cover) and Ray (audiobook) had. Rather than waiting until the draft was done, Jason had been editing along the entire time, and Sean had been managing all of those hand-offs, leaving me with already plenty to do on the morning of Day Twenty-Six as the two of them worked to get my raw Day Twenty-Five words ready for me (again) later.

My job during the polish — which began immediately and lasted until the eleventh hour of Day Thirty — was to watch for consistency and story continuity while adding in all of the stuff we'd added to the book's climax throughout. We call the latter reverse foreshadowing and reverse salting, and it works like this:

Everyone knows how foreshadowing works, right? If a reader is going to find out that a particular character is the bad guy in the end, you'd better allude to the things that make him bad (or the reasons he might sour) a few times throughout the story. If you want there to be an "A-ha!" moment at the apex of your tale; the clues leading to someone's discovery of that a-ha must be in place ahead of time. Done well, foreshadowing should lay out all the pieces for a reader without making what's eventually going to happen seem obvious. In the most suspenseful and mysterious books, you want all the clues in plain sight for all to see ... but only in retrospect, ideally only truly visible to a reader if she chooses to read your book again.

We had a lot of people reading each day's new words as I wrote them, and imagine it made for an interesting reading experience. In the final days, those first readers experienced huge *a-ha* moments that came out of the blue, with no preamble whatsoever.

A-ha! we said. *You could tell it was Atwell outside the Fog because he was carrying his briefcase!*

And readers were probably like, *What briefcase?*

A-ha! we said. *Don't you see? She can tell he's not her father because of what he'd told her earlier! And that line Cora says at the very end, about "crazy" being what happens when you start to believe? Didn't that perfectly recall Eila saying the same thing in the treehouse?*

And readers were probably like, *When did Atwell say* what *earlier?* What *did Eila say in the treehouse?*

For those first people, *The Dream Engine* must've read like a bad mystery novel, where a sloppy author cheats at the conclusion by miraculously pulling something unexpected from his ass. That was because we hadn't done our foreshadowing as we went; we added it later. Only readers of the final book got the full experience.

During that final week with the draft, I had a few things on my punch list:

I needed to split the Ministry of Manifestation into two main departments (Enigma and Aether Forefront). I had to find a way and a place for Eila and her father to discuss her position in Forefront, and for Atwell to deliver the line she'd use later to identify Atwell's doppelgänger in the Fog: "I am proud of you, no matter what you choose." I needed to seed more doubts in Eila about her father's suspicions. I had to similarly sideline Eila and Cora's treehouse discussion to get Eila uttering the line Cora would recall later, when flushing her Crumble at Eila's televised suggestion. I had to add Atwell's signature briefcase, the baker from Eila's childhood who died in the fire, Cora's sketchbook, and more.

That may sound like a lot, but it really wasn't that big of a deal. We believe that good fiction is written in layers, and that it's a massive mistake to feel that you have to get it totally right the first time through. Our job, in the first draft, was to tell the story — to get it out, through all of its twists and turns, until we'd reached The End. Only once the story was fully out could we start to see all of its nuances. For instance, we didn't know Eila was kind of selfish at the outset. But when we went back through, knowing her as we now did, we couldn't help but see her actions through that new lens. Changes dependent on that sort of knowledge were small, but we were always asking questions: *Would she do this this way? Would she say this thing at this time, using these words, knowing Eila?*

Despite having a huge list of things to foreshadow and salt in those few final days (we'd distinguish the two; sometimes you don't truly *foreshadow* a future event but want to *mention* a somewhat extraneous tidbit to add texture — to "salt" it into the draft for flavor), adding them in wasn't really much more work than a normal polish for voice and clarity. For most of our foreshadowing mentions, changes were tiny (in the first chapter, Cora goes from huffing about the Shuttle Shaker ride to huffing while crossing her arms, thus shifting her sketch bag (successfully added — *ding!*) higher on her shoulder) and were no harder than substituting *that* for *which* in a sentence. And so I rolled on, killing the promise to keep my persnickety, meddling fingers out of every other sentence, and made the draft shine.

There were only two places where I had to do significant new work. Together they may have cost me an hour. The first involved derailing a conversation between Eila and her father at the Ministry of Manifestation and bending it into a discussion about Eila's insecurities and Atwell's true feelings about her decision to join Aether Forefront rather than Enigma (two departments I'd made sure to add mention of pages earlier). The second was in the treehouse scene, where Cora had to somehow prompt Eila to say "Crazy is what happens when you start to believe." The second was smaller than the first, but both were simply a matter of massaging the dialogue until I could steer the characters where they needed to go without jarring the reader. It's tricky, but something I enjoy and daresay I'm good at. You can't just interrupt a scene and suddenly have someone say, "Oh, hey, by the way, you're proud of me no matter what I choose, right?" But with practice you'll find ways to hear dialogue while acting as the angel or demon on a character's shoulder, whispering for a slow shift in direction.

Polishing — complete with foreshadowing and salting — is easily one of the most amazing phases of writing for both of us. Depending on how anal-retentive you are (my own AR level while polishing is unfortunately high, but still bearable), you can polish just slightly slower than you'd read, but the change in the draft from that relatively small amount of effort can be breathtaking. Yes, I had to burn a weekend to get *The Dream Engine* polished in time, but it so didn't bother me. The pre-polish book was terrific if you overlooked the climaxes without corresponding buildups, but the post-polish book is a gem.

Small effort. Huge rewards. You want magic? That's it right there, folks.

Day 30 and Beyond

One of the things I can't quite convince my ten-year-old son about (but which is totally true) is that in order to build any muscle, you have to push past your comfort zone. It's true with pushups, it's true with bear crawls and sprints at soccer practice, and it's true with the full array of nonphysical tools: skills, attitudes, fear tolerance, whatever. Pushing those limits is like taking a cold shower before jumping into a slightly less-cold swimming pool: after you've gone to one extreme, anything less feels dimmed by comparison.

Fiction Unboxed had tested us in every way. It tested our nerves. It tested our faith that stories, given room to breathe and enough digging, always have solutions baked into them. It tested our endurance, our pressure thresholds, and our willingness to do something truly different in the eyes of the world at large. It even tested Dave, who did none of the actual writing. Dave is averse to promotion, and fears other people's negative perceptions of him. But by the time it was over, Dave had faced down a few haters during our Kickstarter period to declare, "Fuck them if they don't like it."

In the final quarter of 2013, Realm & Sands churned out more than half a million words. As we considered the notion of writing a novel in a month, improv style, with thousands of eyes upon our every move, Sean and I kept referring back to that 2013 sprint as our training — the time when we'd done all those sprints and bear crawls to prepare for our big June soccer game. But we hadn't realized that *Fiction Unboxed* wouldn't just be the big game. It would also, in fact, turn out to be a brand-new training period on its own.

On Day Thirty, I finished my polish. Sean dotted more i's and crossed more t's, and we compiled the final *Dream Engine* so that we could deliver our newest book to the faithful thousand people who'd watched us write it. Then we stood from our chairs and stretched, feeling weary and strong. Sean had grown an enormous beard in June to help capture the project's real-time nature, and it seemed as if effort clung to his face. He needed a shave. I needed a shower. But we were stronger than we'd ever been, and after a few days off we'd start writing again and prove it.

On the evening of Day Thirty, we held a wrap party for *Fiction Unboxed*, inviting Dave back so we could joke about how offended he'd be at the way Sean and I had "ruined" all his great ideas from the first few days' brainstorming sessions — *if* he ever read it, which we were sure he never would. If I'd ever doubted the enthusiasm or support of the *Unboxed* audience (which I didn't), it would have evaporated that night. As on the opening and closing days of the Kickstarter campaign, the mood was ebullient with team-wide jubilation. The crowd didn't cheer as if Sean, Dave, and I had pulled off something amazing. They cheered as if we *all* had, themselves included.

On Day Plus One, July 1, we pushed a few final buttons and tried to rest. Given the approaching Fourth of July here in America, the rest of the week wasn't especially active. But once the holiday was over we climbed firmly back into our saddles, feeling refreshed and stronger than ever. *Unboxed* hadn't just changed the perceptions of those who'd watched it live and those who continue to watch it non-live today, and it hadn't just changed our own little corner of the writing and publishing world. It had changed *us*. It had changed Realm & Sands, Sterling & Stone, and Platt and Truant. It had changed the *Self-Publishing Podcast*. It had even changed Dave.

The project I woke to on Monday, July 7 was our most ambitious and intimidating project to date: *Axis of Aaron*, a 150,000-word literary vertigo ride that might be at home on David Lynch's bookshelf.

We were actually slated to start *Axis* before beginning work on *The Dream Engine*, but as June neared, I realized that I'd never get it finished in time — or that if I did, I'd have to rush it. I very, very much didn't want to rush *Axis*. Sean's beats for *Axis* were positively beautiful. Reading those beats — wandering the small seaside town of Aaron via carefully chosen photos, meeting Ebon Shale and learning about the recent loss of his wife Holly (who, after her death, Ebon learned had been unfaithful), and meeting Aimee Frey, a girl with her own demons whom Ebon had been infatuated with during three summers as a teen — broke my heart. I wanted to steep in Aaron. I wanted to delve into the strange events that began to unfold as the landscape twisted and warped around Ebon. The project couldn't be rushed. It was all too precious.

Looking back, it's a very good thing *Fiction Unboxed* butted its way to the front of the queue, and that *Axis* had to be postponed. Because before *Unboxed* we hadn't built sufficient muscle to handle *Axis*.

If we'd thought the narrative of *The Dream Engine* was complex, *Axis* made it look like a picture book.

If we'd thought *The Dream Engine* twisted reality, it was only because we hadn't seen the shapes that *Axis* would take. *The Dream Engine*'s twists, à la Daw and his training sequences, formed a knot like a pretzel. But *Axis* inverted space and made an M.C. Escher topology, a Möbius strip with no beginning or end.

If we'd thought *The Dream Engine* required us to have faith that the story would come together in the end, *Axis* flat out had us praying on our knees. I felt like I was juggling unraveling balls of yarn as Ebon's reality split at the seams. Our story meetings were filled with questions like, "So what exactly is real here?" But I never really got those answers, and labored the next morning still not knowing whether I was being fooled or seeing true.

I'd be willing to go so far as to say that *Fiction Unboxed* made *Axis of Aaron* possible.

We'd been forced to articulate our thoughts on reverse foreshadowing in the final days of *Unboxed*. That came in handy as we faced the impossible task of foreshadowing a novel with no truly correct timeline. The rammed-home re-alization that Eila had to change as a character and have an epiphany for our ending to work helped us to see that Ebon, whose reality shifted from scene to scene, needed a coher-ent arc even though doing so often seemed impossible.

Changes we'd made to our writing process because *Un-boxed* required them stuck like thrown pasta on a wall, find-ing their way into our newly evolved way of working — a process we'd been complacent enough to believe was *already* evolved.

During *Unboxed*, we had to record our story meetings so that people would be able to watch, listen to, or read them for years to come. Because they were recorded, I found myself listening back, recalling gems from discussions that otherwise would have been lost. And so going forward, we decided to keep recording our meetings, and during *Axis*, those would've-been-lost gems turned out to be critical.

During *Unboxed*'s final week, we'd had four meetings in five days to untie tangles in our narrative web. We'd had no choice but to hold those meetings immediately because the project's clock was ticking, and in order to make that possible Sean had to edit right behind me as I wrote so he'd always know the story well enough to discuss it. Our old process had me finishing the entire draft before Sean saw a single word, but we found we liked the immediacy of being on the same page story-wise and decided to keep it. When I'd hit a snag like one of those in *The Dream Engine* while writing *Unicorn Genesis* the prior year, catching Sean up enough to even *have* a story meeting about it meant (literally) a monthlong diversion. Deciding to continue the practice of Sean editing right behind me changed that — something that turned out to be absolutely essential for the story that *Axis* came to be. I couldn't have written *Axis* end to end without those discussions. That one change in process meant we could always meet within a day or two, and I could divert to a far simpler "B story" during the lull.

Oh, and one more thing? *Axis* was as improvisational as *The Dream Engine*, giving us a chance to flex those new muscles as well. Sean didn't have an idea for a mindbender novel, then articulate it, then find a book cover to match his concept. What actually happened with *Axis* was decidedly different: We found the cover *first*, picking it out from a set of premade, random-idea covers by a fantastic designer named Jason Gurley. Only then — *once we had a random cover in hand* — did Sean manage to craft our most ambitious story yet.

We spotted character insights in *Axis* that we'd have missed if we hadn't learned how to explain similar insights to Unboxers about *The Dream Engine*.

We saw solutions in *Axis* that would have gone unseen, because *Unboxed* had forced us to articulate every little dilemma and decision.

Our 2013 sprint had made us strong. *Fiction Unboxed* made us stronger. And Axis, piggybacking off of *Unboxed*, made us stronger still.

You'd think that would have been enough and that we'd settle down afterward and rest ... at least for a little while.

But we decided to invite friends over to help us build an entire world instead.

APPLY IT! This Chapter's Takeaways and Action Step

Here's the least you need to know from this chapter:

- Foreshadowing is essential to a well-told story, but it doesn't have to come in the way that most writers believe it does. It can arise at the end, after the foreshadowed event finally occurs, and then get seeded backwards during a later draft.
- Writing is an iterative process. You want to make each layer of the process — each draft, in other words — stronger than the one before it.
- To build muscle, you must push past your limits and do something that scares you a little.

And here's something you can do RIGHT NOW to apply this chapter's lessons:

- Take something you've previously written, then go through it again, reverse foreshadowing events that will happen later. Don't overdo this. Keep the mentions small — just enough to keep a reader's eye on the ball without revealing too much or going for an overly dramatic reveal. Then watch the magic happen.

PART THREE: *BUILDING A WORLD TOGETHER*

CHAPTER TEN:
The Story World Summit

Funding *Fiction Unboxed* through Kickstarter forced us to stretch beyond our comfort zones. And true, some of that stretching was superfluous and felt like frittered effort on ineffective activities ... but plenty of it did what stretching is supposed to do, and made us grow.

We had to clearly articulate what *Fiction Unboxed* was so the Kickstarter community would accept it. Without that pressure, we'd have done a poorer job with our sales copy.

We had to make a video for our Kickstarter page, because projects without videos always flop. Making that video was a migraine and led us down several dead-end paths before we found the right one, but as with the sales copy, that process forced us to launch the project's from its best perspective. The video's final script was orders of magnitude better than the first. The video's positioning ended up influencing the project's theme, turning it from "Watch us write a book" to "Change the world with a story." Even the video's music altered how we approached our campaign. We'd wanted a soft and thoughtful score, but Garrett argued vehemently to use our up-tempo *SPP* introduction music instead. He was right, and the project's energy ramped up dramatically as a result.

But most importantly, the Kickstarter campaign forced us to think BIG.

If we wanted to make waves with the project, it had to be vastly overfunded — a way to make it newsworthy and keep it visible as a landmark in the Kickstarter top rankings. And if we wanted the project to look like a normal, reasonable Kickstarter, we had to offer a wide range of backer rewards rather than the scant few that originally occurred to us: $5 for the finished book, $19 for transcripts, $49 for an all-access pass, and $297 for participation.

Luckily, those two challenges had the same solution: We needed to offer some big-ticket backing levels to increase funding and neatly fit with what the Kickstarter community considers normal — even if nobody bought them. And if we were going to *offer* premium levels, we had to develop rewards that were remarkable enough to justify their price tags.

The process, as we neared launch, worked opposite a typical product development flow. Usually you come up with a product or service, *then* decide on its price. We did the inverse. We already knew the price levels required to round out our campaign, so we turned our attention to figuring out ways to make them amazing instead.

That meant hiking up our britches. Prior to *Fiction Unboxed*, the largest single sale either of us had ever made for something we'd created was just under $1,000, and selling something for a grand is no small feat. How were we supposed to justify anyone spending twice that much for the $2,000 level? Or *five* times as much? Or *ten*? We knew we wanted to use Kickstarter's full span of possible rewards (from $1 all the way up to $10,000) — in part to show the indie world what was possible for the little guys and gals, in part to stretch ourselves personally and in part to anchor the lower-tier backing levels as the bargains they were. But we couldn't ask anyone to pay for champagne without showing them the bottle. We're ambitious, not assholes.

We scratched our chins. What was worth $2,000? What was worth $5,000? And what about a novel-writing project, pray tell, could possibly be worth $10,000?

Then the answer dawned on us.

Travel, here we come.

A Long Haul to Austin

Sean and I have — together and separately — attended many live events. Some have been inexpensive and others have had us digging through our couches for pennies. But no matter how much an event cost, every one has been worth it. We've attended conferences as a by-the-way and come home with amazing new contacts with whom we've later ended up building great new things. We've learned strategies through casual conversations, then returned to implement with tremendous effect. Our first-of-its-kind author website was built after a conference. We've come home with new book covers. New plans. New friends. New and unprecedented levels of inspiration.

The best thing you can do for your business is to meet with smart people in your field face-to-face, breaking bread and sleeping under (or at least near) the same roof. For us, time is the most important asset we could possibly offer.

If we wanted to give maximum value to our project's highest-tier backers, it meant spending time with them over the course of days, helping them to grow alongside us.

We decided to implement something we'd slated as a "someday maybe" idea several years ahead of schedule: a small group, in-person event, somewhere between a conference and a mastermind group. We called it the Story World Summit, and broke it into two sessions. The first — called the WorldBuilder Session — would be open to a dozen attendees and take place just two and a half months after *Unboxed* wrapped. The second (our Colonist Session) would be held six months after that, open to twenty-four attendees.

We weren't just going to plop these people down in a VFW hall and lecture for hours. What we had in mind was far, far more intensive than anything typically termed a conference. We planned to work with attendees for two days, building a story world we'd all live and work together, brainstorming co-promotional ideas, sharing meals and drinks and the very best of our brains. It was called Story World Summit for a reason: We were creating a world collaboratively, summit fashion, helping everyone in attendance to craft an outline and idea for a novel in this brand-new world that was complete enough, compelling enough, and in line with the world enough to start writing immediately. We didn't want to broadcast to a large group then *hope* they'd learned something. We wanted to get our fingers into their clay and their fingers in ours. We wanted a small, focused group of motivated authors who'd go home and write a book, series, or serial that would expand the world's reach and benefit everyone in attendance.

Accordingly, the Summit's backing levels on Kickstarter broke down like this:

Our $5,000 backers would attend the Summit's World-Builder Session, held in Austin, Texas, on September 13 and 14 of 2014. The group would be limited to twelve attendees, and the books we outlined at the event would be considered canon to our world, meaning those works made the rules that everyone else writing in the world would have to follow. We'd promote those canon works through our site, our podcast, and in our books themselves. We'd organize a bundled promotion that included everyone's first-in-series works, thus threading our efforts like hair in a braid. We'd pay for all attendees to stay in Austin's beautiful Renaissance Hotel; we'd pay for their food; we'd treat them to an amazing formal dinner. We had their backs, from end to end. And "we" also meant *all three of us* because even Dave, who hates to travel, promised to make the trip.

The Colonist Session, at $2,000, was meant for writers who loved the power behind the WorldBuilder Session but couldn't manage the price tag. We knew we could transfer the most amazing, most beneficial things about the WorldBuilder into the Colonist Session with minimal loss by framing it slightly differently. Colonist attendees' works would be "near canon" but not quite canon, meaning they would establish some world rules but have less impact due to the fact that their footsteps would tread the world's soil once the world was six months more mature, and following many of the first WorldBuilder novels release. The group would be twice as large, and Dave wouldn't promise to attend, making the us-to-them ratio somewhat smaller but still high-touch. We couldn't swing hotel fees for Colonists, but they'd still have two intensive days' worth of our highly focused time, our support, our detailed help with their outlines, our network, and a way to shape the world we were all building together.

The only thing we could think of to justify a $10,000 spend was to take the WorldBuilder and plop several weeks of Sean's time atop it. So for those highest-level backers, Sean would comprehensively edit and polish their work as he'd do with any of our own — something that he won't do now, regardless of the price, and regularly turns down. We'd buy those backers an excellent book cover, write their product description, have them on our podcast to promote their book, and a bunch of other little superchargers.

If you're looking at those price tags and thinking we have some big-ass egos, you're absolutely right. We were saying to the world that our focused time was worth around $100 per hour for the Colonist Session, or $250 per hour for the WorldBuilder. (Those figures are actually overstated — each session carried significant expenses, and we'd be splitting what we made three ways — but we'll ignore that for now.) But that's actually part of the point. Anyone looking to make an impact and do amazing things *has* to think big, and too many artists think small because that's how most artists have been trained. *Embrace* your ego. You have one anyway if you're a writer, because writing means you feel that the world should care about what's in your head. Shoot for the moon with your book, your works, your business. And so, true to our word, that's exactly what we did.

This should be obvious, but the fact that we'd created those high-ticket Kickstarter levels didn't mean anyone would buy them. We had access to nobody's wallets; we didn't promise OMG NINJA KINDLE MILLIONAIRE TRICKS TO MAKE YOU RICH; we didn't even hold guns to any loved ones' heads. Our strategy was simple — and, frankly, the only one our ethics would have allowed. We delivered the idea, explaining what attendees could expect, along with what they absolutely should *not* (i.e. bestseller status or instant riches). Then we announced the idea and let our audience decide. If people believed in us, trusted us, and thought they'd get good value from the Summit, they'd sign up. If they didn't, they wouldn't. Worst-case scenario: Sean and I would force Dave to drive from [REDACTED] to Austin, and we'd all finally get to meet each other in person, which we'd never done before.

In the middle of May, about two-thirds of the way through our Kickstarter funding period, Sean and I flew to Denver to attend the first-ever Authority Intensive conference hosted by our good friends at Copyblogger — a big copywriting and marketing blog that gave us both a huge push when we were brand new to writing online. We love everything about Copyblogger, from their chops to their ethics to their insistence on doing everything to the nines.

Our goal in attending was simple: We weren't speaking; we weren't in need of a conference's worth of new information (we had too many ideas already); we weren't trying to network or make connections. We simply wanted to hang out, see our friends, shake Brian's and Sonia's and Chris's and Robert's hands and congratulate them on their conference. Those goals were easy to meet, and we met them within hours of arrival. The rest of the trip was gravy.

That first night in our hotel room (we'd split one to save money; there was no financial gain to be had by going, after all), we found ourselves thinking about Copyblogger's conference and our own Summit. We wanted to have our own crew, and get people as excited about flying to Austin as we'd been for Denver. And yet, at the two-thirds mark of our campaign, no one had picked up a ticket. Dave was happy because he hates travel, but we were sighing. Had we actually thought anyone might be willing to pony up that kind of cash to sit with us and strategize? It had sounded so great on paper, but maybe we'd been deluding ourselves. Oh well. At least we'd offered the levels — thinking big and filling the campaign's sidebar at the same time.

At about 11:30, we were about to sign off the Internet and get some sleep when Sean refreshed the page "just one last time" and saw our first WorldBuilder attendee.

The next night, *also* right as we were about to sign off, we saw our second.

There we were, together at an in-person event, getting back-to-back registrations for our own in-person summit. It was the only time during the campaign that Sean and I were even in the same city ... and bang bang, we'd just got two registrants in one tiny window. It was as if we were *meant* to do this.

People believed in the project. They believed in *us*. We climbed an Everest of emotion.

Pack your bags, bitch, Sean texted Dave, giddy. *The Summit's on, and it's a long haul to Austin.*

Going in Empty

In the end, we had five attendees for the WorldBuilder Session. Surprisingly, we'd only had a single taker for the Colonist Session (although we expect that number to increase quite a bit; as I write this, the Colonist Session is still six months away). It was strangely flattering. Even though attending as a Colonist cost 40 percent of the WorldBuilder price, those who chose to attend were choosing to "attend all the way." It was a level of trust — and hence responsibility — that we felt marrow-deep. These people didn't just *believe* in what we were doing with our still-young company. They believed it *all the way*.

Sean lives in Austin, and the lush Renaissance Hotel is only about ten minutes from his home. I hadn't made my imminent move to Austin yet and thus had to fly down, but I did so with my wife and kids in tow. The plan was to toss our two families together and allow them to bond so that everyone would be eager and prepped for our inevitable move. We arrived about twenty-four hours before the attendees and planned to leave thirty-six hours after our Summit responsibilities were over. And so as soon as we arrived, we began filling time. And waiting.

We had hours to burn and weren't sure when our attendees would arrive. Dave, who hates flying and enjoys self-flagellation, made the twenty-hour drive from Florida and wasn't due in until late. And so once we'd taken my kids hiking (to see some exciting lizards) then dropped them into the able care of Sean's wife, Cindy, Sean and I didn't know what to do with ourselves. We paced the nearby shopping center, detouring through a high-end furniture store called Restoration Hardware as research for an upcoming story. We got coffee and paced some more. Then we plunked down into a set of couches in the lobby, the weight of what was coming pressing down upon us like the ten-story hotel wrapping the atrium above.

We discussed our business.

We planned an upcoming online course.

We hashed plot on an upcoming story, and leafed through the Restoration Hardware catalog, mining ideas.

Finally I said, "So we're going to plan the second *Dream Engine* book this weekend too, alongside everyone else planning theirs."

"And the third," added Sean.

"So what ideas do you have for the books?" I asked. Because that's how we work, and how we'd handled the first *Dream Engine*. Sean conjures the big, loose ideas, and I fill in the details. The process had been rushed in June, but Sean had an advantage this time because he could plan ahead. He didn't have to wait until Day One to start brainstorming as we'd done during *Unboxed*. And because the coming weekend was all about getting our core series to agree with the books our attendees were writing, I knew he'd have most of the plot of our second book in mind already. How else could we possibly build a shared world with our attendees? But also true to form, Sean had yet to tell me his ideas. I was eager to hear them, and now, while we killed hours, seemed like the best possible time.

"None," said Sean.

I sat up and stared at my white Russian as if to say, *Did you just fucking hear him say what I heard?*

"None?"

"None."

"You have no ideas."

"Nope."

"For two books. That we're expected to map out this weekend. So that the people who paid us all that money can outline *their* stories in ways that agree with the rules our books have established. The books that haven't established *any* rules yet because you have no ideas. Just tell me if I'm getting any of this wrong."

Sean had a margarita. He sipped it, then settled back. "That's all correct."

For about ten seconds, this realization was scary. Then I realized that it wasn't scary at all; it was, in fact, stuffed with faith, just like all of *Unboxed*. If Sean had already mostly outlined our second book in his head, we'd have been safer. We'd have known that *our* story, at least, wouldn't fail to gel as we were juggling the stories of our attendees, trying to make *them* come together. But although it would have been safer, it wouldn't have been as rich an experience for the Summit collective as allowing our books' ideas to germinate *alongside* their books — to nurture our books' growth in the collective world rather than to hamstring that growth by establishing too much of the world in advance. So yes, going in empty was a great idea ... assuming, of course, that it worked. Assuming our outline *could* come together from nothing in two days while we were giving the majority of our attention to the attendees' stories.

I took a drink. I slouched back to match Sean. I wished Dave was there. I'd never met Dave in person; I'd experienced his wrath and curmudgeonry only through a computer. I love Dave, but I was also a bit afraid of him. One more thing to be nervous about.

"Sounds like a plan," I said.

It took hours for our attendees to show. We'd more or less cleared Friday afternoon, knowing that people were arriving around that time but having nobody's schedules. We waited. We talked. We sat. We walked. We sat. We talked. And finally, we went for an early dinner at a tapas place near the hotel. I let Sean order. We got an appetizer trio and an order of brisket tacos.

As we were finishing, Sean's phone finally buzzed with a text.

It was Kalvin, our first to arrive.

Eight Minds, One World

Kalvin spotted us first, as we were walking through the hotel's atrium. We all sat together at the lobby's Starbucks clone and tried nudging what we'd taken to be a reserved guy from his shell. But Kalvin's shell didn't last long, as he rattled off a long line of extremely impressive ideas for stories he already had in the works.

Sean and I exchanged a glance. We hadn't known these people especially well ahead of time, and Kalvin hadn't even been very vocal in our online communications. There was always a chance that our attendees would turn out to have questionable ideas that might conflict with what the world was trying to do, but Kalvin put those fears to rest immediately.

Matt came next, closely followed by Amy. We moved into the bar area, but shortly after ordering our first round of drinks, Monica and Garrett arrived. Dave came last, because that's how show business works: You save your big act for the end, allowing time for maximum excitement to brew. Sean and I were the opening act. Everyone really wanted to see our resident "I hate you all" grumpy guy ... who, in person, turned out to not be grumpy at all.

The group gelled incredibly well from the start. It was astonishing, and an excellent sign of what the next two days would offer. We ordered a few flatbread pizzas, a few beverages. Most of the attendees ordered only water and soda, making me — a guy who has maybe two drinks a month — feel like a lush. And Garrett, being our resident filmmaker, recorded it all in case the Summit turned out to be like Pixar's first meeting or something.

We made our introductions, thus handling in advance a huge swatch of time we'd planned for Saturday morning. Our group was an ambitious, qualified, highly motivated, and energetic lot. Most had extensive experience writing (and some copywriting) already — all except for Matt, who made up for his freshman energy with easily the most passion and drive in the group. Matt had just made a career change and said more than once that he considered writing to be his destiny and our meetup to be "the chance of a lifetime." He'd pounded his stakes in the ground, determined to publish his first book — in our new, shared world — by the time he turned for, then just a handful of months away. Over the next five years, he'd write another twenty-five. But unlike when most people say such outrageous things, it was impossible to doubt him. Matt was positively vibrating. The man was ready to run through walls.

By the time we adjourned for the night, we were already bonded. This was to be the Alterra dream team. This was the strike force that would forge boldly into the unformed, malleable world and make it amazing. We hadn't volleyed a single story idea, and yet could already sense the truth: the world of Alterra was in excellent hands.

We met the next morning in a lushly appointed board-room that made us feel much more professional and with-it than Sean, Dave, and I actually are. The conversation was slow to get going as we all woke up, but began to escalate dramatically as we decided on our world's first key market-ing strategy: a box set containing everyone's first-in-series books — including *The Dream Engine* — that we'd make per-manently free as a loss leader designed to draw new readers into the world's funnel. (If that last sentence's jargon con-fused you, it's basically like when the store gives you free samples in order to entice your purchase.)

This plan excited the room. We exchanged ideas for how to make it work better. Someone pitched the notion of all our books having similar covers to unite them under a single brand, and someone else had a list of possible design-ers to fit the bill. Amy was already editing a collection of Al-terra-world stories; she pitched ways to make the collection work for us as well.

The room was buzzing by lunch. I'd had my doubts about how well a group of eight could cocreate anything, but those doubts were already disappearing.

The biggest thing on Sean's, Dave's, and my mind was making sure the experience fully delivered on our attendees' desires. So we racked our minds — and flat out asked them

— to determine not what we'd set out to give them ... but what would benefit them most.

Building the world, they kept saying.

We'd mapped an agenda in advance, breaking each day into an hour-by-hour schedule that rotated between formal world building for Alterra, instructional content (how-tos on character arcs, series versus serial construction, etc.), marketing, planning, and breaks. That agenda was a memory fifteen minutes into the morning. We had to follow the room's flow, shifting between curtailing less-juicy rabbit holes and recalibrating our efforts toward what our five attendees wanted most and could benefit maximally from.

Kalvin, Matt, and Garrett wanted to write stories outside of Alterra's borders. The first *Dream Engine* book had taken place entirely inside Alterra, and only at the very end does the reader learn that there is, indeed, a world beyond the Fog. We'd mentally pictured Alterra as being a fictional version of the United Kingdom (minus Ireland; sorry, Ireland), and that meant the rest of the fictional Earth was up for grabs. Our three men were all ready to plant their flags in outlying territories, each claiming one for himself.

Monica and Amy both wanted to write books inside Alterra itself. That meant we had to split our time between setting the stakes for the planet (and what was to come as that big spaceship Eila encounters at the end of *The Dream Engine* declares its hegemonic intentions) and more clearly spelling out the rules of Alterra itself.

Because we'd informally imagined Alterra as being the UK, Sean and I had thoughts on where each of our fictional cities was located. But we hadn't formalized any of it, so on Day Two we set about making a map. Dave drew the UK on a huge presentation tablet, and I plotted cities, laying them mostly atop existing locales.

Waldron's Gate sat atop true London.

Manchester became our Vatican City of Thestic.

The military city of Stensue was located at Edinburgh.

And we plonked the asylum, Joffrey Columns, down on the Isle of Man to isolate it and keep the rest of the population safe from Joffrey's insane. (But to heighten the coolness, we allowed the Fog to surround the Isle's bay, thus giving the Alterrans there what would appear to be a huge lake.)

We added cities where they seemed to naturally fit, ignoring the real-world map. The northernmost city of Yon was placed high in Scotland, with only rural lands beyond. The abandoned and supposedly haunted city of Aerohead went a bit farther south and very close to the Fog, with the superstitious little berg of Nascent nearby. And on a whim, we decided to drop the city of Alseer on England's large southwestern peninsula. There, everyone felt, the Fog should actually be out in the ocean rather than right up against the land. That way, Alseer could be a beach vacation spot, where Alterra's rich had their vacation homes.

Then we pivoted, fleshing out the rest of the world. Every continent would have its own machine like the Blunderbuss, we decided ... but only Alterra's would still work. That, of course, inspired envy in the rest of the globe, and made them eager to get their hands on Alterra's Lucky Charms. But it wasn't apples to apples anyway; all of the machines, when they'd been functional, had worked differently. Australia's (which Matt renamed "Kona") stole and manipulated souls, creating death cults and a race of reapers. The machine in Africa ("Biafra") swapped the essences of animals into humans, giving them powers. Asia's machine converts life energy into chi and creates waste in the form of atmospheric and barometric disturbance. And

North America's ("Nova") stole resources from the ground to meet the nation's needs. As the Novans built their sci-fi ships and armadas, they weakened the continent, eventually crumbling it into the ocean and turning their population into well-armed nomads.

The energy ramped up. And up. And up.

On Saturday night, after an almost obnoxiously fancy dinner at a Brazilian steakhouse that everyone except Dave and my ten-year-old son loved, Sean began to outline the first *Dream Engine* sequel based on the group's brainstorm. He brought it in Sunday, and we took turns adding to our outline as well as the attendees'. Amy's and Monica's books intertwined with ours, because half of the second *Dream Engine* book would take place inside Alterra, where Monica would be playing host to the insanities at Joffrey Columns and Amy would be weaving a nest of spies from our previously innocuous Ministry of Decorum. Garrett's, Matt's, and Kalvin's stories *also* meshed with ours, because the other half of our next book would take place outside of Alterra, with Eila, on and around the giant Novan ship. We had to establish which chess pieces were in motion on the global stage, what the stakes were, who might win, and why.

I knew that TV shows and movies were written in groups, but even after cowriting with Sean for a year and a half, I couldn't imagine how that would work. How could so many cooks stir a single pot of soup? Wouldn't they trip over each other? Wouldn't they get in one another's way?

No, they wouldn't. If the group blends well and is talented enough, the resulting brew creates synergy rather than discord. The result is greater than the sum of the group's parts. I'd already known, from writing with Sean, that one plus one could equal three. What I didn't realize until the Summit was hitting its apex inside that little boardroom was that eight ones added together could equal twenty. Thirty. Fifty. More.

By the time we wrapped on Sunday evening with a final round of food and drinks at a nice Italian restaurant, we were a unit. Friends. Collaborators, all intent on a mutual goal — all of us in it for the long term, all of us enthusiastic, none of us in an unrealistic hurry.

What's worth doing is worth doing well.

And working together, Alterra was in excellent hands.

Dave 2.0

Dave, either uncharacteristically optimistic about the trip or loathing the start of his long drive home, decided to stay the same extra day that my family had already committed to. We bid farewell to our five attendees Sunday evening, then Sean and Dave met up again Monday morning to catch up as a working unit as I'd done with Sean before Dave's arrival. We'd already been planning to move (part of the trip's purpose was to warm my change-averse son, fortuitously also named Austin, to the city and Sean's kids), but being there had won us all the rest of the way over. So Monday morning we drove by homes we might like to live in, then headed downtown to walk the shops on South Congress and detoured to a donut place called Gordough's, where heaven awaits.

Everyone — Sean and his family, Dave, and I and my family — gathered later on Monday for a Dave-style dinner including fried cheese, then played a game called Telestrations before breaking up for the night. Our families went to bed, and we very much wanted to do the same. We were spent. But regardless of the fatigue, there was still one important thing we'd yet to do.

Despite being together for three days, we hadn't sat as an exclusive trio. The three of us talk for several hours each week, and had yet to have an in-person conversation alone.

We made our homes in comfortable lobby chairs. Sean got another margarita. I got another White Russian. Dave got a Diet Coke. And while the bar's pianist crooned in the background, we took our final few hours to decompress. As a unit. As the Three Musketeers, our jobs successfully done.

Sean asked if we thought the attendees felt they'd got what they'd paid for. We agreed that yes, they all certainly seemed to. They'd said as much several times over that final shared meal: that we'd exceeded their expectations. That we'd started something amazing together. That we'd always remember the Summit, because it was the first. The beginning.

It felt great to believe all of that, because we'd spent so much on the event that our profit had been hacked in half. But it didn't matter even a tiny little bit. Even if we'd lost money, it was worth it to start something, to forge bonds with such an outstanding group. For the three of us to finally sit in a small circle together, feeling the simmer of great things to come.

"So, tell the truth," Sean said to Dave, "was this miserable for you, being away from home?"

Dave said it wasn't. Not at all. Not even a little tiny bit. We'd grown used to Dave bitching about being away from his house and his faithful Target and his many nemeses who work there, but he'd had fun. On the podcasts, Dave's most common expressions are exasperated or good-naturedly angry (yes, there is such a thing). But our curmudgeon spent his weekend smiling. Even when we ambushed him at Sunday's lunch, telling our waiter it was his birthday and that everyone would need to come over and (loudly) sing.

"I'm excited for next year's WorldBuilder," he told us.

And there was more. If there was sufficient interest in the Colonist session — enough to exceed the twenty-four slots of our limited registration — Dave said he'd be willing to come back for that one. He wasn't booked for the Colonist Session, but if we wanted to invite thirty-six attendees instead of twenty-four, we'd need to add a third instructor to maintain our ratios. And let's face it, everyone ... Dave isn't equal to Sean and me in "meet the guys" power; he's superior. Fans *accept* me and Sean, but they really all *want* Dave.

We called our new, Austin-bound Dave "Dave 2.0." I was already planning my family's move to Texas. Shockingly, the same inkling seemed to be growing in Dave.

We sat in the hotel lobby and talked. And talked. And talked. Past midnight, despite our fatigue.

We'd never felt better about our partnership. We'd never felt better about the future of independent publishing (or, more globally, indie storytelling), and vowed more than ever to stay at its bleeding edge. We'd be uncomfortable out there, doing things that more and more people thought were crazy. But that, it turns out, is where you'll find much of life's sizzle.

Sean, his eyes drooping, rose from his seat, finally willing to kill our pow-wow.

"I can't believe it's over," he said.

But that was kind of bullshit.

It had only just begun.

Get Smarter Faster (FOR FREE!)

**"Write. Publish. Repeat"
Conversations**

The Smarter Artist, #1 Amazon
Bestselling Authors, Podcasters, ...

★ ★ ★ ★ ★ (12)

WRITE. PUBLISH. REPEAT. **CONVERSATIONS** is a 30+-part instructional video series (retail price $49) in which the authors elaborate on the cutting-edge things learned in self-publishing since releasing the book version of their #1 bestselling guide *Write. Publish. Repeat.* in 2013.

Visit the link below to get the *Write. Publish. Repeat.*
Conversations course for FREE!
SterlingAndStone.net/Repeaters

Want to Learn on the Go?

HOW WOULD YOU LIKE to learn in your spare time with **hundreds of hours of FREE CONTENT** that will help you get smarter faster? Hear us answer our most frequently asked questions, discuss the latest ins and outs of our business, offer secret peeks at our creative and entrepreneurial process, conduct interviews with authors, artists, and industry leaders, and give you **FREE audio versions of our books and stories.**

Visit the link below to discover your new favorite (FREE) audio addiction NOW!

SterlingAndStone.net/podcasts

Do You Want to Know What it Was REALLY Like?

To download your FREE Fiction Unboxed extras like the unedited transcripts, first morning video, our original story notes PDF, and links to the 30+ blog posts published throughout our adventure, or to find out more about the full Fiction Unboxed experience, The Sterling & Stone World Building Summit (all sessions), or what's next in the Fiction Unboxed adventure, please click or visit the link below.

SterlingAndStone.net/unboxedextras

We Need You

Reviews are essential to our growth.
If you enjoyed this book or found it helpful (especially if you were part of the original *Fiction Unboxed* project), we would love it if you took a moment to leave a review on Amazon or Goodreads.

A few sentences is plenty, just enough to let fellow readers know what you liked about the book.

THANK YOU IN ADVANCE. WE APPRECIATE (AND COULDN'T DO THIS WITHOUT) YOU!!

About the Authors

JOHNNY B. TRUANT is a speaker, co-host of the top-rated Self Publishing Podcast, and the author of well over 2 million words of popular fiction.

Johnny, along with partners Sean Platt and David Wright, also launched the *Fiction Unboxed* project in 2014 ~ a record-setting Kickstarter after which Johnny and Sean wrote a full-length novel in 30 days, starting without any ideas or genre, in front of a live audience, sharing every detail of the process including story meetings, emails, and raw story drafts. The novel birthed through *Fiction Unboxed* (*The Dream Engine*, first in the Blunderbuss/Alterra series) went on to spawn what the Sterling & Stone team calls "open-source fiction": an open story world in which any author may write and publish without requiring permission and without paying royalties to the world's creators.

Johnny's fiction works (mostly co-authored with Sean Platt) include the political sci-fi serial *The Beam*, the fantasy/western mash-up *Unicorn Western* books, the satirical *Fat Vampire* series, the literary mindbender *Axis of Aaron*, and too many others to count.

Johnny, Sean, and David host their trendsetting, boundary-pushing podcasts every week on the YouTube, iTunes, Stitcher, and their cornerstone independent author website at SterlingAndStone.net.

SEAN PLATT is a speaker, founder of Sterling & Stone, and author of more than five million words of published fiction. Together with co-authors David Wright and Johnny B. Truant, Sean has written the series *Yesterdays Gone*, *WhiteSpace*, *ForNevermore*, *Available Darkness*, *Dark Crossings*, *Unicorn Western*, *The Beam*, *Namaste*, *Robot Proletariat*, *Cursed*,

The Dream Engine, Invasion, Greens, Space Shuttle, and *Everyone Gets Divorced,* the traditionally published titles *Z2134* and *Monstrous,* and the standalone novels, *Axis of Aaron, Crash, 12,* and *Threshold.* Sean also writes for children under the name Guy Incognito and has more of his share of nose.

Sean lives with his wife and children in Austin, Texas, and has more than his share of nose. Follow him on Twitter at @seanplatt.

DAVID WRIGHT is one half of Collective Inkwell, a publishing company specializing in dark fiction and serialized fiction. Inspired by Stephen King's serialized story "The Green Mile" Wright and co-author Sean Platt set out to bring serials back into fashion in summer 2011 with their post-apocalyptic serial, *Yesterday's Gone,* which has since been followed by dozens of other books, serials, and series.

When he's not writing books, David can be found writing about writing and pop culture at his blog at DavidwWright.com. In his "off-time" he can be found chasing his five year old around the house, cleaning up a cat whose sole talent is producing prolific amounts of hair and poop, or ranting about stuff as his wife rolls her eyes.

In September 2012, the writing duo signed a deal with Amazon Publishing's 47North to write two Kindle Serials, *Z2134* and *Monstrous.*

Sean, Johnny and Dave, also hosts several podcasts on the Sterling & Stone podcast network. You can see the full lineup of shows at at http://sterlingandstone.net/podcasts, and easily subscribe on iTunes, Stitcher, or wherever you prefer to get your podcasts.

What We've Written